TONE DEAF
IN BANGKOK

AND OTHER PLACES

BY JANET BROWN
PHOTOGRAPHS BY NANA CHEN

Tone Deaf in Bangkok
By Janet Brown
Photographs by Nana Chen

Cover and book design by Janet McKelpin/Dayspring Technologies, Inc.
Editing assistance provided by Robert Tompkins

Please be advised that restaurants, shops, businesses, and other establishments in this book have been written about over a period of time. The editor and publisher have made every effort to ensure the accuracy of the information included in this book at the time of publication, but prices and conditions may have changed, and the editor, publisher, and authors cannot assume and hereby disclaim liability for loss, damage, or inconvenience caused by errors, omissions, or changes in regard to information included in this book.

For information regarding permissions, write to:
ThingsAsian Press
3230 Scott Street
San Francisco, California 94123 USA
www.thingsasian.com
Printed in Singapore

ISBN-13: 978-1-934159-12-5
ISBN-10: 1-934159-12-3

TABLE OF CONTENTS

I. Introduction   4

1. Careful, You're Speaking   8
   of the City I Love

2. Second Childhood   14

3. Becoming a Guava   20

4. Tone Deaf and   26
   Tongue-Tied

5. A Refuge from "Polite"   30

6. Nausea and Desire   38

7. Learning Thai   44

8. Envying Travelers   54

9. Ghosts In the   60
   City of Angels

10. Shopping 101   68

11. Survivor   72

12. Suvaporn's Daughter   80

13. Food for Every Mood   86

14. Three Seasons   92

15. Toilet Paper   96

16. Escapes From   100
    Bangkok

17. Among the Living   106

18. Today, Where   116
    Do You Go?

19. All Dressed Up With   122
    No Place to Go

20. Drowning In   126
    the Deep End

21. Skytrain Tourists   134

22. Going Home Again   140

23. A Few of My   146
    Favorite Things

24. Fireweed and Jasmine   152

Author & Photographer   156

INTRODUCTION

I have spent most of my life searching for a home. Taken to Alaska at an early age by parents who were fulfilling their dreams, I knew as soon as I was fully conscious that the frozen north was not the place for me. Always restless and discontented no matter where I was, I grabbed the chance to live and teach English in Bangkok as soon as it was offered to me.

There, in a city that was unlike anywhere I had ever been, I grew to feel that I had at last found what I'd wanted. After the bewildered frustration of my introductory months, when I sobbed my misgivings into letters to my patient family and friends, I slowly realized that Bangkok, with its peculiar mixture of hedonism and industriousness and *joie de vivre*, was where I was meant to be.

Unfortunately, it wasn't where my family was meant to be, and that cold, hard truth turned me into a human ping-pong ball, returning to the States every two years or so to be with people I loved. Now living in Seattle, I'm carefully planning my final journey to Bangkok, where I plan to remain until the day I die.

Like almost every expat in Bangkok, when I'm asked why I like to live there I babble something vague and incoherent about the light, the food, the people, the climate, and the lack of earthquakes, which is a major strong point to someone who has always lived on a fault line. If pressed to go beyond that glib litany, I answer with a mosaic of facts: the beauty and ugliness that co-exist side by side, the warmth and humor behind the omnipresent masks of smiles, the irrepressibly free spirit of the city that is often regulated, but never with any lasting success. Then I get lost, in the scent of jasmine and the stench of garbage, in the shrill piercing of the whistles of security guards as they direct vehicles in and out of their domains, in the blazing colors of temples, in the frustration of being caught once again in the traffic jam of memory that traps me when I think of Bangkok. So I tell stories on paper, searching for the people and experiences that have made this place one that has captured me and held me and kept me in love, hoping to bring other people there who will learn to love it too.

An inhabitant of two countries, I have deep gratitude for people in each one. In the States my thanks go to my editor and dear friend, Kim Fay; my publisher and friend, Albert Wen; and my first readers and friends, Alison Boyce, Bridget Boylan, Leah Brock, Jane Darrah, Peter Melman, Holly Myers, Tamra Nisly, and Tracy Taylor. In Bangkok, my heart, as well as my thanks, belongs to Worasak Jongthirawong; Eddy and Usa Chanthakan; Jessia and Rodney Moore; with appreciation going to Jim Algie at *Untamed Travel* magazine. And always, wherever I may be, all of my love and hopes and dreams are with the men who are my sons, Matt and Nick Brown.

THIS BOOK IS FOR JANET MEEHAN,
MY MOTHER, WHO ALWAYS KNEW WHY.

น้ำขึ้น FLOOD

1 CAREFUL, YOU'RE SPEAKING OF THE CITY I LOVE

I live, at this point in my life, in the ideal American city. Seattle is small enough to be friendly, large enough to be urban, and is surrounded by enough natural beauty to launch a million calendars. Its inhabitants can walk to work, drink the tap water, and pass by a dog without worrying that it might be rabid. It's a city without dengue fever, avian flu, malaria, or leprosy. The temperature rarely goes above ninety degrees or much below freezing. Tourists come to the bookstore where I work, raving about this place, and it takes everything I have to keep from saying, "Thanks. Glad you like it. It bores me silly."

I can't help it. I've been warped for life. I've given my heart and whatever might pass for my soul to a city that is infamous around the world for its sin, pollution, and political chicanery. It's such a filthy place that I've scraped dirt from my skin while sitting in an apartment fifteen minutes after having taken a shower, and I've had to pick my way down neighborhood thoroughfares to avoid stepping in dog shit. The air tastes like a cigarette and frequently smells far worse. Most people can't wait to leave it, and I can't wait to return. Yes, it's true. I'm thoroughly besotted with Bangkok.

Like all lifelong relationships, this one has its flaws. It certainly wasn't love at first sight or a whirlwind romance, and I've tried to file divorce papers more than once, but I've always come crawling back.

Bangkok is vibrant, and for me that covers a population bulge of sins, much in the same way that the perpetually increasing jungle of green vines covered the garbage that blanketed the vacant lot below the window of my first apartment there.

That lot was a gathering point for taxi drivers with bursting bladders, and I frequently opened my curtains upon arising to see a small line of them energetically peeing. It was a piquant sight to gaze upon while drinking my first cup of coffee in the morning, and I found myself waving to them insouciantly while muttering, "Good morning, boys. How's every little thing?"

This spot was also my building's unofficial garbage dump. From the apartment windows, tenants tossed out plastic bags of refuse that were visible for a little while, and then were swallowed up by the green vines. It was an efficient arrangement and gave me for the most part a very rural and attractive vista, until the day that I awoke to see a gigantic double bed mattress reposing on top of all the greenery.

Rodney dropped by with my mail to find me in a state of angry, hysterical sobbing. "Look at this," I demanded, dragging him to look at the huge, stained, hideous addition to the neighborhood, "Just look. It's going to take months for the vines to cover that up."

The next morning I steeled myself, took my coffee over to the window, looked out, and began to laugh. Below me were several dogs, mangy, scabbed, and monstrous, running and bounding and leaping, having the time of their lives, playing on that mattress that was as grisly as they were and that was obviously born to be a trampoline for repulsive canines. At that point, an odd little shift occurred in my perspective, and laughing seemed to be the most valid response to many of Bangkok's little surprises.

That discovery came in handy when the rainy season began, and I learned how to say *flood* in Thai. There were a vast number of them during my first year, and I became accustomed to taking off my shoes, pulling up my skirt, and wading knee deep down what had been a city street a few short moments before but was now a lake filled with people who were walking through water while smiling. It was an inconvenient, dirty, and quite possibly health-threatening experience, but the people around me were reacting as though it were a snow day, and I learned to feel that way too.

Laughing gave me a horde of female Thai friends one night, when I stepped backwards while being introduced to a large group of women, and got in the way of a gigantic fan that immediately began to devour my long, full skirt. It had captured several yards of silk that covered my lower body until one of the women turned it off, and it became quickly obvious that the fan and I were now as one.

"You will have to take off your skirt," said one of the women, but since we had only just met, I countered with a suggestion that I thought was more appropriate, "Why don't I carry the fan home with me and I'll return it in the morning?"

Since the fan was almost as large as I was, that suggestion was as amusing to all concerned as the first one had been. One of the women brought me a beer, and I tried to look nonchalant as I leaned against the fan, drinking my chilled Heineken, and realizing just how thoroughly ridiculous I was capable of being.

"Oh, let's just cut the damned thing loose. I'm tired of it anyway," I pleaded. Somebody cut me free so carefully that the rip, when mended, was virtually invisible, and I didn't lose a skirt, I gained a tableful of friends, all of whom called me Fanny.

Women were the ones who opened the heart of the city to me and showed me how to live there. Thai women are beautiful, smart, strong people, and many of my friends are so cosmopolitan and worldly that I never spend time with them without feeling as though I should be picking the hayseeds out of my hair. I'm not the only American woman who learned from my Bangkok counterparts that it was possible to be independent and capable while still being feminine and that strength in every gender can coexist with tenderness, which is a valuable and sometimes difficult thing to learn.

"You are not beautiful," my friend, Arun, once told me, "but you have a strong charm." It's a phrase that I think of often when I think of my chosen city, rarely beautiful but always compelling. And yet in the middle of ugliness that is so profound that it becomes fascinating, beauty flickers in a persistent flame. It can be seen at night when light and shadow transform a polluted canal into gold-sparkled, deep purple splendor, when twilight deepens every visible color in that instant or two before the disappearance of the day, when the music of chanting monks fills the grounds of a temple and erases the blaring city outside, when the sun rises above the low-hanging mist that cools the city's first light, when the Royal Barges float in endless procession, turning the Chao Phraya into a river of regal magnificence.

The most impossible question between lovers—"Why do you love me?"—cannot be answered in a simple twenty-five words or less. It's always so much easier to enumerate those things that make love less than perfect; curses are sometimes more frequent than endearments. When I think of the many times I've cursed and complained about this city, it's strange for me to realize that my most enduring and joyful relationship has been with Bangkok, and I only regret it took me so long to find this place that I'm convinced is mine.

HELLO

2 SECOND CHILDHOOD

Nothing is more humbling than being forty-five years old and suddenly discovering that you are unable to read, except perhaps being forty-five years old and struggling to learn a new alphabet taught by small children who correct you each time you open your mouth.

Believe me, I know. I arrived in Bangkok as a fully functioning, although thoroughly exhausted, adult woman and woke up in a world that took me straight back to pre-literacy. I didn't realize it immediately, since I was a guest in a household that spoke fluent English and possessed what I, in my naiveté, regarded as basic essentials of everyday living: a coffee grinder, Italian roast coffee beans, and a daily newspaper (in English, of course.) Then I ventured beyond the walls of my hosts' courtyard, and the fun began.

I had few expectations of Bangkok, beyond the belief that I'd be living in a city. Every picture I'd seen of my new home was decidedly urban, befitting a metropolis of eight to ten million people, but the world that I walked into was certainly not like any city I had ever seen before. I was on a narrow street that was filled with trees, houses, a cluster of small shops, a large covered market, and many hideous dogs that all looked like promising candidates for euthanasia.

Rodney, whose house I was staying in—the man who had offered me a job and would eventually become my brother—took me out for my first meal in Thailand, to a dark little place for noodles. When I reached for the salt, he said, "Careful. That's not what you think it is." He handed me a bottle of fish sauce and took away the sugar before I sprinkled it on my food.

Rod was an American who could speak Thai, and I was in awe. I'd listened futilely to language tapes before my arrival and had bogged down in the first few minutes when I was unable to hear the differences among the five tones that characterized every Thai word. It was no easier now that I was listening to actual conversations, and when we finished our meal, I retreated to the unequivocal pleasures of a cold shower and a long nap.

I woke up in the afternoon feeling confused and disoriented. On our morning stroll I'd seen a sign in English that said "Sugar Moon" and I had absolutely no idea what that was supposed to mean. Our street had a strongly rural flavor, but it was right beside the headquarters for Thai Airways, with its high-rise buildings that were as tall and as contemporary as the ones I'd left behind in Seattle. We had stopped on our way back from breakfast to buy water and milk, which Rod purchased at one of the neighboring houses, and when he told me the Thai words for these things, they sounded identical. As a person who hated milk, and had drunk approximately five gallons of water since I had arrived in Bangkok the night before, I was beginning to feel a little worried.

"How difficult can this be?" I consoled myself, and then decided, "I can learn this language." With this firmly in mind, I asked Rodney to teach me how to say *hello, excuse me*, and *thank you*. It was easy enough to replicate those sounds, and I felt confident that I could present myself to the general public as a polite simpleton, although the feminine ending of *ka* that completed every phrase made me feel that I was impersonating a cockatoo.

I was prepared to spend some time savoring my new vocabulary acquisitions, but Rodney urged me toward the door. "Come on. We're going to buy you a bus map," he informed me, "and an alphabet book."

We stood at the side of the road, facing an approaching pickup truck. Rodney's hand moved palm downward in a languid gesture, the truck stopped, and we climbed into the back, which was canopied with a long bench running down each side to accommodate passengers.

Our journey ended at the beginning of what was my idea of a city. The trees and houses had disappeared, replaced by crowded sidewalks and concrete buildings and steep metal staircases that led up to pedestrian overpasses near an elevated highway with twists and curves. It all looked as though it had been designed by a devotee of M.C. Escher, someone with a penchant for metal and cement. I had never seen anything quite so ugly or so completely fascinating.

Rodney whisked me down a street of women who were selling piles of fruit and food that I had never seen before. We passed a jewelry store filled with gold where a small child lay napping on the counter, the familiar sight of a 7-Eleven that was embellished with a mountainous display of cosmetics at its entrance, and a man sleeping in a hammock that was tied to the supports of the highway that roared overhead. We moved through the sound of a thousand lawn mowers from the street beside us, as countless small motorcycles zipped through the sluggish stream of cars and buses, many of them carrying women who rode side-saddle behind the driver. I stared in disbelief as I saw one of those women, mirror in one hand, lipstick in another, court certain death by applying makeup in heavy traffic.

It was a noisy, grubby, incoherent scene that we rushed through, and I was completely enchanted by it. Then we entered a cool, multi-leveled, brightly lit cavern that was the size of several football stadiums and contained one of Bangkok's busiest shopping centers.

The escalators were clogged with an ocean of white and navy blue uniformed teenagers, and women chicly clad in black. Each floor extended farther than I could see, with a dizzying array of shops, and rising above it all was a mammoth TV screen that blared pop music.

A bookstore containing books that I couldn't read had a bus map in English, and an alphabet book illustrated with cartoons that were so garish that I didn't want to touch it. After making these purchases, we went back to the spot where the pickup truck had dropped us off. There were no trucks waiting there, but a cluster of motorcycles was parked nearby and Rodney grinned at me and asked, "Do you want to take a motorcycle taxi home?"

Remembering the women I'd seen earlier, I hoisted myself up in side-saddle position and we headed down the narrow road away from the traffic and into the trees. Back in the tranquil safety of Rodney's court-yard, I collapsed into a chair, and tried to assimilate everything I'd seen.

"The women are so elegant here. They all wear black, just like in New York," I remarked to Rodney, clinging to the one observation that made sense to me.

"They're in mourning for the King's mother, who died last week. They'll dress that way for a month or so. Otherwise they don't wear black; it's the color of death," he informed me.

I began to mentally review the clothes I'd brought with me, many of which were black, and felt a spurt of gratitude that I had "a month or so" before I had to jettison my wardrobe. I wondered where I would ever find clothes that would fit my American body in this country of legend-arily slender women, realized it was too much for me to consider at the end of my first day in Thailand, and went back to bed.

The house was empty when I got up the next day, and I spent the morning trying to replicate the ornate and complicated characters in my new alphabet book. My efforts were dismal, and I made generous use of an eraser. Sud-denly Rodney's car pulled up, and out tumbled a circus of little children.

They were delighted to find me poring over the alphabet, since it was some-thing they had all mastered years before. Each was eager to teach me the forty-four characters and determined to do it before the afternoon was over.

The most insistent teacher was a five-year-old boy, whom Rod had nicknamed the Generalissimo. While his older siblings eventually gave me up as totally untrainable, Ooh was made of sterner stuff. I still have nightmares of him leaning into my face, with his small features in an expression of mingled determination and menace, carefully enunciating words that I could never repeat to his satisfaction. I'm certain that we would still be together in some horrible Sartrean hell, if Rodney hadn't rescued me by suggesting that it was time to get something to eat.

Soon after that, I realized that I had to get a place of my own. The comfort of Rodney's house, with its walled-in privacy, the large bedroom that I slept in with its screened windows and giant fan, the burgundy-tiled bathroom where clean towels magically appeared, courtesy of his housekeeper, and its freshly ground morning coffee, was seductive, but it was not mine.

I had a lot of work to do, I knew, before that degree of comfort was something I could claim, and being insulated by it at the outset of my time in Bangkok was a handicap. Rodney took me down the street to a building called Rainbow Mansion, which was ornamented with columns and classical statues that were heavily influenced by that well-known scholar of antiquity, Cecil B. DeMille, and enveloped by a verandah that Scarlett O'Hara would envy. It contained apartments that were far less elaborate than the building's exterior would lead one to expect: single rooms, with miniscule attached bathrooms, whose focal point was a double bed, accessorized with a desk, dining room chair, clothes cupboard, and a hideous little brown plastic loveseat. There was no kitchen.

The room that I rented was gloomy, which I realized was probably a positive quality in a country of perpetual sunlight, and faced a large vacant lot, which was covered with a small jungle of brilliantly green, fast-growing vines. It was horrible, it was mine, and with a newly purchased fan, a little hotpot, and a jar of instant coffee, I was ready to explore the pleasures of an unaccompanied life in a city that I hoped would someday become my home.

3 BECOMING A GUAVA

Farang, the word for foreigner, as every foreigner in Thailand rapidly learns, is also the word for *guava*, which means that it's a word that lends itself easily to puns and all sorts of merriment. This is certainly appropriate because foreigners are a source of vast entertainment and often feel that they must be starring in a live-action Thai national sitcom called *What Will That Crazy Farang Do Next?*

It didn't take long for me to understand that I would never be Thai, but it was harder to figure out that I would become a resident of Thailand only after I got over the feeling that I was American. Any Thai neighborhood worth its salt can strip away that notion in a few weeks, particularly from foreign women who come there alone. This experience, although sometimes painful, is essential for anybody who would like to live in the Kingdom.

A particularly unpleasant acquaintance of mine summed it up nicely when she informed me that I lived in Thailand, not America, and shouldn't behave like an American. Unfortunately, by the time that I'd received that useful nugget of information, I'd already absorbed it through hard-won experience, with the result that I dressed more conservatively and spoke much more softly than my informant did. But then she was sheltered by the privileges of citizenship.

I was a fast-walking, fast-talking, eccentric, middle-aged woman when I first arrived in Bangkok, with the deep-seated belief in individual freedom that was my American birthright. I was thoroughly out of place in my new neighborhood in the deepest suburbs of Bangkok and that fact bothered me not an iota, although it should have.

I soon met a group of women who were Rodney's friends. They hung out at a lovely little garden restaurant where they drank beer, smoked cigarettes, and wore Levis. "My kind of people," I decided and responded, "I guess so," when one of them asked if I was a tomboy. "What an odd question," was my immediate internal reaction, and then I forgot about it.

I rushed around Bangkok with the careless speed of a person who has always had enough space, and looked with amazement at Thai women who walked as slowly as though they had just learned how. I found a rock and roll club far from my neighborhood, and before my first visit asked Rodney what I should wear. "Oh, black and Levis," he advised me, and so every weekend I'd put on my jeans and my black pullover and stay out until 2 a.m., always awakening the apartment building's security guard when I'd walk past him early in the morning.

I learned to drink beer instead of Scotch because it was cheaper, and I learned to smoke from my friends at the restaurant. "Thai women don't smoke in public," I was told and thought, "I'm American," and inwardly scoffed at the idea of sneaking my cigarettes.

So there I was, a woman who did everything she pleased, in public, who didn't realize that "tomboy" was Thainglish for *dyke*, and that smoking on the street was what prostitutes did. I was definitely pushing the limits of local tolerance, and I was beginning to get the impression that I was living in the wrong neighborhood. People weren't smiling at me as much as they used to, and the pickup trucks that served as buses on our street often didn't stop when I tried to flag them down.

I made a vague attempt to discuss some of this with my apartment manager, who had a serviceable command of English, but she didn't seem to understand what I was talking about. I shrugged off the feeling that all was not well and went on with my life. Maybe after my visa run to Malaysia, I might look for another place, but there was no rush, I told myself.

I came back with my favorite kind of souvenir, a good story, and I called Katrin, my one American female friend, to tell her all about it. It was a train flirtation, a couple of kisses, an exchange of phone numbers, very teenage and silly but a nice little anecdote. She laughed and I laughed and that should have been the end of it, but it wasn't. The next time I went out of my apartment, my tropical little street had turned glacial.

People looked at me; nobody smiled. Vendors fell silent as I walked by. I was served food at a noodle stall without a flicker of the basic baby-talk conversation that everybody knew I was capable of. Worst of all, I could hear my name frequently in jovial conversation that took place in the courtyard of my apartment building at night, in combination with words that I could understand like *train* and *Malaysia*. When I walked down the street, I frequently felt like *Ryan's Daughter*, that shunned and shorn violator of convention, and wondered when I would lose my hair and how the whole story had gotten out in the first place.

I was lucky, during that dark period, not to know what I later learned from Arun. His father had once shaved his older sister's head because of behavior that he thought was shameless, and Arun himself, when he became head of the family after his father died, had done the same thing to his younger sister when she misbehaved.

I heard men's voices catcalling under my window late at night, and the next day I fled to Rodney's house. He had left for the States the day after my return from Malaysia, and, bereft of his guidance and protection, I took refuge behind the high, sheltering walls that surrounded his yard.

I finally found a new place to live in another neighborhood and stopped in at my apartment to begin to pack my belongings and to telephone Katrin to chat about what my future home was like, and where it was. I left quickly after hanging up, and as I was going down the stairs to the courtyard, I could hear the apartment manager standing near the office telephone where she connected incoming calls to the tenants. She was gleefully revealing the name of my new building and the name of my new neighborhood to a woman who worked with her, and I realized she had, with her competent English skills, been monitoring my phone calls. Suddenly everything became clear to me, including how to keep this from ever happening again.

This is how I became a guava: I started to pay attention to how things were done and how people behaved, and I began to learn. I dressed the way that my professional female students did, and I walked as slowly as they did, and I learned to murmur when I spoke Thai. I didn't go out at night unless someone went with me, and I never smoked on my street. I made a studied attempt to blend in, and to learn how to follow all of the rules so I could later figure out how to break them.

My new neighborhood loved me. I was their very own farang, who was trying hard to learn the right way to behave and was so funny in my attempts; yet because I was trying, their laughter was gentle, and they did their best to help me get a clue.

Much later, and after much assimilation, I was discussing my Bangkok initiation with Rod.

"But the women at the restaurant all smoked and wore blue jeans and drank beer, and they're good Thai women," I said, still puzzled by the varying behavior codes.

"For one thing, of course," he explained slowly and carefully, "they're lesbians. For another thing, they don't behave that way outside of the restaurant. That's their safe place where they can do what they want." As a farang, and another kind of outsider, I found this made perfect sense.

Back in the States, I'm still a guava, walking too slowly on American streets, speaking in a murmur when I order food in Thai restaurants, feeling a quiet little thrill when I walk outside dressed in whatever clothing I happen to be in the mood for. I want to keep as much as I can of my guava-state intact and ready to wear for the time when I once again resume my life as a farang in Bangkok.

4 TONE DEAF AND TONGUE-TIED

Any language in which the words for *fear* and *salt* are differentiated only by a smile is one that had to have been constructed by people who possessed well-honed senses of humor. I tried hard to keep this in mind while I struggled with the intricacies of the Thai language, committing the crime of *lèse-majesté* every day as I cursed King Ramkhaemhang of sainted memory, that very funny guy who invented the Thai alphabet.

I knew I was in trouble on my third day in Thailand when a friend cautioned me to pronounce the alphabet character *kor kwaii* with a long vowel sound. "Otherwise," he cautioned, "you'll be saying the word *penis*, not 'buffalo.'" This preyed upon my mind quite a bit, because I frequently traveled to teach a class that was in the neighborhood known as Saphan Kwaii, and the thought of telling a motorcycle taxi driver that I wanted to go to Penis Bridge was not one that filled me with great glee.

There was a strong possibility that any attempts I might make to speak Thai would result in instant humiliation of the worst kind. Rodney once related an anecdote that paralyzed my vocal cords every time I thought of it. While traveling with a group of female friends, he asked one of them to pass him his sunglasses. Not only did his request go unfilled, every one of the women began to shriek with hysterical laughter. Not until much later was he able to corner one of them and force her to confess that he had asked not for sunglasses, but for an extremely intimate area of the female anatomy.

Stories like this confined me to safe and bland phrases like *please, thank you*, and *where is the toilet*. I massacred even these simple locutions with my engrained American insistence that tone of voice should convey emotion, not meaning. Rodney tried to convince me of the importance of tone by telling me about the time that he called his best friend's mother a "dog" but that was more quelling than it was encouraging.

I refused to order my favorite meal because I had been told that the wrong tone could throw it into the realm of unspeakable obscenity, and almost burst into tears when I discovered that the words for *far* and *near* were identical sounds of one syllable, distinguished by a single tone.

Even in English translation, the diabolical humor that formed the underpinning of the Thai language was loud and clear. Once I went to dinner with a group of students, all bankers, who took great pleasure in ordering a dish that was called "Your wife's little sister." There was no safety anywhere; the refuge of my very own language contained pitfalls when it was used in the Kingdom of Thailand. *Milk* and *eggs* could provoke wild laughter in a classroom of children, since those words in Thai meant "breasts" and "testicles." *Key* if pronounced in the wrong tone meant "excrement," and I would go to extraordinary lengths to avoid any discussion that might involve water buffalo.

When I wasn't struggling to avoid obscenities, I was presenting myself as a complete half-wit. By the misuse of a simple vowel sound, a friend informed me, I was announcing to taxi drivers "I live here," rather than "Stop here," in front of such unlikely domiciles as supermarkets and nightclubs. One of my pretty little students was beginning to detest me because my faulty tone turned her nickname from "Bee" to "Potbelly," much to the unrestrained amusement of her friends. Another student, a gorgeous man with a lovely sense of the ridiculous, was helpless with laughter when I introduced him as being ugly instead of as my pupil. I stopped complimenting people on their babies when I found that I was saying they were bad luck when I meant that they were beautiful. Perhaps my crowning achievement in mangling the language was when

I told a friend that he had a dog's mouth, rather than a gift for sugared speech, and I still don't know how in the hell I managed that. I would be, I decided, a much more likable human being if I just wandered silently through Bangkok while clutching a well-used bilingual map in one hand and pointing with the other.

My friends all assure me that English is much more difficult than the Thai language, and that may well be true. Thai grammar is a cinch to learn, the letters of the alphabet carry one sound each, and only one, unlike the *c* for cat, *c* for city, or the *through*, *bough*, *enough* nightmare that plagues our own twenty-six characters. Thai, however, is more perilous than English has ever dreamed of being, and if you don't believe me, just try asking any Bangkok motorcycle taxi driver to take you to Saphan Khwaii.

5 A REFUGE FROM "POLITE"

Nice girls don't. Ladies never smoke on the street. Always wear clean white gloves when you go out. Eye shadow in the daytime is vulgar. Shoes should cover your toes unless you're on the beach. Always be sure that you wear a slip and that your skirts cover your knees. These were American social rules for women that were repealed in the '60s and that I was sure I'd never abide by again. Then I moved to Thailand.

Rodney had told me that he dressed for work in Bangkok as if he were going to a job interview, so I had brought suits and long-sleeved silk blouses with me in an attempt to dress for success in the classroom. That was "polite" clothing, my students all remarked approvingly, but it was sweltering and at the end of a long workday I felt as though I'd spent eight hours in a sauna. Then a friend gave me a pretty little sleeveless shell to wear under my suit jackets, and although it was a shade of green that made me look like old cottage cheese, I loved it and wore it as often as possible.

I woke up one Sunday morning with a full day of leisure stretching before me, and when I reached for my customary appropriate clothing, something within me rebelled. I left my apartment wearing a full skirt, the green top, sandals, and best of all, no stockings.

"I'm American today," I announced to friends as I left my neighborhood. They looked surprised and a little shocked, but that was undoubtedly because they had always seen me encased in a suit, stockings, and black high-heeled pumps, I told myself. Later when I was stared at on the buses and in the streets, I attributed that to being a foreigner and ignored it.

I roamed happily through the city, scrupulously avoiding temples and palaces where I knew my clothing would be considered "impolite." It was a good thing that I enjoyed my day of sartorial freedom because it was my last. That evening when I went to dinner at my favorite neighborhood restaurant, everybody told me how sexy I looked, and that was when I learned that in Thailand bare shoulders were an erotically charged body part.

Things have changed since then, and today sleeveless blouses are conservative compared to the halter tops that are frequently seen on the streets of Bangkok. In the mid-90s this was definitely not daytime street attire, and after discovering that, I turned to my female students for guidance.

They were all executives and mature women who had worked their way up in banks and corporate head offices, so I figured they were the right people to ask. Everything they told me was oddly familiar, since it was exactly what my mother had taught me in mid-century America, and I soon became pathetically grateful that at least I didn't have to wear white gloves.

Months later, my "becoming a guava" episode taught me that conservative clothing would not be enough unless I modified my behavior as well. "My daughter saw you in the supermarket yesterday," a student, part of the female advisory group whom I privately called my Thai mothers, told me. I, who had yet to meet her daughter, braced myself to keep from visibly recoiling. I began to feel slightly mad, as though I had nowhere to hide from constant scrutiny, and behaved as though I were perpetually under camera surveillance, unless I was in my apartment, alone. I was well on my way to becoming a farang version of a Thai middle-aged woman, the kind who responded to "How was your weekend?" by saying, "I watched TV. I slept."

Before I launched my shopping expedition to obtain a TV and several high-necked, long sleeved, floor-length nightgowns, I met Eddy. He was a friend of Rodney's who had been hired to staff the office of Rod's fledgling language school, a smooth-faced Bangkok charmer in his twenties with fluent English and a flicker of bad temper lurking behind his radiance of smile. Rod wanted me to refine Eddy's creatively flawed English grammar, but soon the time that we spent together became far more conversational than instructive.

Eddy's life was one long episode of *Sex and the City*, with a new foreign boyfriend every weekend. "But," he assured me, "I'm not one of the S&M boys—they're out for sex and money. I'm F&F—fuck and forget." Accustomed as I was to the careful polite discourse that I had with my students, I was delighted by Eddy's frankness about his adventures, which we would discuss instead of grammar points during our scheduled classes. He was, I discovered, a beguiling mixture of impatience, kindness, and perception that was almost extrasensory, and I was fortunate that we became best friends.

My life had become so guarded and circumspect that my chats with Eddy were true therapy. It became obvious that we could say anything to each other, and suddenly a part of me that had been smothered by "polite" behavior codes could breathe again. Eddy would drag me out of the office for lunch in the neighborhood, and since he was completely unconcerned about public attention, I began to abandon my solemn and formal nun-like outer shell.

Thailand is a country that is blessed with three New Year celebrations: December 31, when people exchange gifts and count down to midnight; the lunar Chinese New Year, with its firecrackers and lion dances, when many of Bangkok's businesses are closed; and *Songkran*, the traditional Thai New Year, in mid-April.

What I had heard about Songkran was that what had begun as a time to pay ritual respect to elders by bathing their hands with water had become a country-wide water fight when people jovially attacked each other with water Uzis and fire hoses and buckets of water for several days. The more I was told about this, the more determined I was to flee the Kingdom and not return until sanity was restored. Eddy however had other plans.

"Come with my friends and me to Khao San Road for Songkran," he said, a week before my intended escape.

"I hate Khao San," I replied, which was perfectly true. Khao San was the center for backpacker tourists, notorious for its fleabag guesthouses, its cheap beer, and the even cheaper travelers who slept in one and drank the other. It was a tourist slum that most Thai people avoided as strenuously as I did, and I was surprised that Eddy asked me to go there.

"You won't at Songkran," he assured me. I was intrigued enough to wonder why not and, since Eddy refused to help me make the reservations that would allow me to fly out of the country, I said, "Okay. I'll go there with you."

I met Eddy and his friends, Tommy and Em, on the day that Songkran began, and we piled into a *tuk-tuk*, Bangkok's iconic form of public transport that resembles a large golf-cart with a canopy and a long seat behind the driver for passengers. Khao San Road was unrecognizable when we arrived. The sidewalks were covered with tables, and there was no room for traffic on the street, which was a raging water-battle zone. Foreign travelers and Thai residents were united as a community of Rambo impersonators, stalking each other with plastic machine guns filled with water and attacking in vicious commando raids, saturating everyone within firing range.

Somehow, in this horde of waterlogged maniacs, Eddy managed to find his mother, two sisters, and his aunt, and then an empty table outside a bar that became our base camp. Equipped with our own portable water artillery, and many bottles of water as an ammo stockpile, we settled in to drink beer and defend our territory.

Thailand's social control has now extended to Songkran on Khao San with regulations that determine the kind of music that issues from the bars and that keep the sidewalks table-free, but at the end of the twentieth century it was pure, festive anarchy. The most outrageous participants were those people who lived under the Kingdom's rigid code of "polite" behavior. As one who had submitted to that code and was suffocating as a result, I learned that the insanity of Songkran's water fights was a liberating counterpoint to the stifling propriety I'd assumed for months. Taking Eddy as my model, I smoked and drank and flirted and hurled water as recklessly as he did, ignoring the more decorous example of his female relatives, who sat and watched with benign amusement.

At the end of the day, my clothes were so soaked that I felt as though I'd been trapped in a washing machine with no spin cycle. I was prepared to slosh my way home with Eddy's mother and sisters, but he grabbed my arm and said, "No, you're coming with us. Em has clothes that will fit you." So off we went to Em's apartment, where I was given a pair of his slacks and a polo shirt. The guys changed into tank tops and skimpy little shorts and we left for Soi 4, the gay nightclub area off Silom Road.

The *soi* had been transformed into a combination of Weimar Republic Berlin, Niagara Falls, and Mardi Gras. Torrents of water cascaded over bodies so creatively covered with garments that I gaped without shame. One tall beauty with a mane of auburn poodle-curls and pants that appeared to be lacquered on impossibly long legs sauntered down the flooded soi as though it were a catwalk, accompanied by a companion who was identical except for a blazing-pink, sculpturally layered wig. Another gorgeous creature was clad in short strings of jasmine blossoms that made the shortest mini skirt in the history of the world, with a loop of jasmine around each wrist as bracelets. In my slacks and shirt, I was the one who looked, and felt, like a female impersonator.

The nightclub that Eddy, Tommy, Em, and I squeezed our way into was a claustrophobe's nightmare. A maelstrom of bodies gyrated on the dance floor, and the energy of the dancers took over the room as much as their physical presences did. Every bit of space was as packed as a bus during Bangkok's rush hour. It was impossible to smoke without burning the person standing closest to me, and taking a sip of my beer put me in danger of being perilously close to knowing my neighbor in the Biblical sense.

"So many people," I shouted to Eddy.

He smiled and said, "Oh, it's always like this."

Eventually Eddy would teach me how to feel at home in a club where I was the only source of natural estrogen, but that night I felt like E.T., a friendly and rather unsightly alien. I was tired, one of my sandals was hanging by a thread, and the relentless thud of disco music was making my head throb. "It's only 1:30," Eddy protested when I told him I had to go home, but he guided me through a maze of people, out of the club, and into a taxi.

The city was a mist of aqueous impressionism, an unfamiliar blur of neon and water. I shuddered as the taxi driver assured me that Songkran was much more fun up north in his hometown of Chiang Mai than it was anywhere else in Thailand. Shivering in my wet clothes while my sandals slowly dissolved into leather mush, a happy survivor of Bangkok's diluted version of Songkran, I silently vowed never to brave Chiang Mai's superior waterpower.

"I was with my friends," was my demure and "polite" reply when my students later asked how I had spent Songkran. They all nodded approvingly, while I congratulated myself on having learned that skillful editing is the secret of living in Thailand. Later, when I walked through streets filled with expressionless, quiet, public faces, I'd smile and think, "Go ahead, be "polite." I know better than to think that's who you really are. I've seen Songkran in Bangkok."

สมาคมพ่อค้าผ้าไทย
泰國紗布商公會
THAI TEXTILE MERCHANTS ASSOCIATION
ร้านจรุงกิจ
CHARUNGKIJ
622-4181-2
HKS
MOTOR SPORTS

6 NAUSEA AND DESIRE

The covered market that I walked through every day on my way to work was one of my favorite places until an odd smell emerged that refused to go away. Actually it was more of an olfactory assault. I had become accustomed to the different stinks and fragrances that reached my nostrils all at the same time and had learned to enjoy the process of sorting them into their various categories: refuse, canal water, jasmine, heated garlic, freshly squeezed oranges, and bus exhaust fumes. This, however, was not an odor that I'd ever encountered before; it was rotting and putrid, and it permeated the air for blocks in the covered market. "Sewage," I decided as I rushed through the miasma of stench, handkerchief over my nose and mouth like a gas mask.

One night I stopped at a noodle stall in my neighborhood and as I was finishing my meal, the owner approached me with what appeared to be a large chunk of yellow bath sponge resting on a plate. "For you," she announced, handing me the plate and a spoon, and standing beside me with a broad and expectant smile.

I took a spoonful of this mysterious object, which had a soft and creamy texture like an extremely solid mousse. As I raised the spoon to my mouth, I had to force myself not to gag. There, inches away from my taste buds, was the stench I encountered every day, and there, inches away from my elbow, was a woman who appeared to be quite happy to have given it to me. I put the spoon in my mouth.

It was the most seductive flavor that I had tasted since the moment I'd first sampled a ripe and oozing Brie. It was sweet and luscious with a faint hint of something that was vaguely corrupt. It was decadent and I wanted more.

"Durian," the shop owner told me, and suddenly I understood what this object was.

Durian is a fruit that looks like a prehistoric weapon designed to kill *Tyrannosaurus rex*. It is the size and shape of an American football, although a darker shade of brown, and is covered with long, sharp spikes. One man famously described its flavor as "eating ice cream in an outhouse," and it was banned from planes, trains, buses, and almost all hotels. It was a delicacy, my students told me later, and its best varieties were well beyond the reach of an ordinary budget.

It was also extremely rich and several mouthfuls were all that I was able to eat. I looked wistful as I told my benefactress that I was full, and she wrapped it in many, many layers of plastic, secured the package tightly with a rubber band, and told me to take it home to eat later.

My apartment was a basic one and I had no refrigerator, so I put the plastic-swaddled durian on a little table and went to work on lesson plans. Suddenly I realized that my room smelled like a market, and what I smelled was certainly not flowers.

"Impossible," I muttered to myself as I tentatively approached my hermetically sealed chunk of durian. When I picked it up and sniffed it, it was indisputably the source of the offending odor, and when I quickly put it down, the smell clung to my hand.

The durian had to go, but it was a gift, and delicious, so I didn't want to callously toss it into the garbage. Turning to the phone, I called one of Rodney's housemates, Scooter.

"I have a durian but I can't keep it in my room," I told him. "I'll bring it to you so you and Rodney can have some—it's wonderful, but you know how it smells."

"No," he shrieked into the receiver. "You cannot. I hate durian and so does Rodney. Throw it away."

It was a sad moment as I wrapped the plastic lump in still more plastic, and as guiltily as I would dispose of a dead baby, I crept outside to the trash barrel and carefully jammed the durian under a large pile of discarded newspapers. Perhaps, I consoled myself, someone would smell it and take it away to appreciate it. I hoped whoever that might be would not be the generous noodle stall owner or any of her acquaintances.

When friends discovered that I liked durian, they made sure I was well supplied. They also told me to be careful. Under certain circumstances this fruit could be lethal, and not only for the unfortunate Malaysian woman I read about in the paper who was killed by a durian that fell from a tree while she was strolling through an orchard.

"Never eat durian and drink beer; you will die. Durian is a hot food and so is beer. Your stomach cannot stand that much heat."

When I discovered that this toxicity extended to Johnny Walker Black as well as to beer, I ate durian well before cocktail hour and prayed that every trace was well digested before someone might offer me a drink. This strategy worked better for me than the somewhat dubious solution that Eddy offered. "Eat lots of mangosteen if you have beer and durian. Mangosteen is a cool food and it will keep your stomach from getting too hot." That sounded too much like the Caterpillar's advice to Alice in Wonderland when he told her to eat one side of the mushroom if she wanted to grow and the other side to shrink. Alice had difficulty fine-tuning those instructions, but all she had to worry about was size. I had a little more than that at stake, so avoidance seemed the best policy.

Then one day I ate durian before getting on a bus to go to class. The afternoon was warm, the bus was crowded, and as I stood clinging to the side of a seat, an unmistakable scent began to perfume the air. It was too subtle to be coming from a chunk of the fruit, and with a feeling of dread, I bent to sniff my forearm. Exuding from my pores was the ghost of what I had eaten an hour earlier, and I was enveloped in a fog of embarrassment and durian.

After that, I only ate durian in the early hours of my day off and satisfied my craving for it at other times with durian ice cream, milkshakes, and dried chips. These all lacked the full power of the original, while conveying enough of its memory that neither Scooter nor Rodney could be prevailed upon to share them with me.

The hazardous quality of durian wasn't confined to the joys of the table or the dangers of wandering under one of its heavily laden trees. One morning I was rushing mindlessly past a spot where two old women threaded roses and jasmine to make garlands and sold a small quantity of fruit. I was wearing a flowing, full silk skirt and it became caught on something as I hurried by the pile of produce. I tugged at it, and turned to see that I had pulled a durian from the pile, which became mobile as it was released from my skirt and rolled slowly and inexorably down a slope into a canal. The old women and I stared in horror as it sank into the dark, murky water and shuddered at the thought of retrieving it. "Where are the children?" one of the women asked, but the little street urchins, who usually populated the area, and who could be persuaded to do dirty jobs for a few baht, were nowhere to be seen.

The solution was obvious to us all. The durian proved to be exceedingly rare and expensive, and I was in no position to question that assessment. I paid, the women waved me off to work, and I walked past them with extreme caution from that day forward, while they smiled and asked without fail if I wouldn't like to buy another durian.

There were other kinds of Thai food that marked me as an indelibly foreign object: *bpla rah*, the fermented fish that was meant to be used sparingly as a flavoring agent but which I ate, only once, in a large spoonful as though it were peanut butter; steamed silk worm larva, which tasted as though I'd bitten into a vitamin capsule, bitter and nasty; fried whole caterpillars, which were crunchy and salty like popcorn but stuck between my teeth, made my stomach hurt, and prompted memories of reading about cows on the Great Plains who ate caterpillars during a time of infestation and died. I could never manage to eat the tiny whole birds that were deep-fried with their little heads intact, although I'm sure they are every bit as good as the fried frogs that I liked to eat before going to see a boxing match, and I'm still haunted by the memory of the skewered whole field rat that was the focal point of a neighborhood stall one morning. For me, however, none of these things will ever be as irresistible and dangerous as durian, which I never think of without pangs of deep respect and longing.

7. LEARNING THAI

"I haven't felt the way you do for a long time," Eddy said on the afternoon before Wit's visit. "You're nervous about what's going to happen and what you're going to say."

"I am not nervous, "I protested.

"You will be," Eddy assured me.

"I'm never nervous with Wit. He makes me happy when he walks into the room, and we always have something to talk about."

But I was nervous later that evening and babbled for hours, up to the moment when he asked, "May I kiss you now?"

"Oh, yes," was my answer.

Several months before, I had been searching for someone who would help me learn Thai, and Crazy Peter the Pothead said he had a friend who could. The friend turned out to be a tall, slender young man dressed in job interview clothes, who met me in the lobby of the bank where I taught. We introduced ourselves in formal and stilted English, and then I broke protocol by asking him to join me for a beer.

We negotiated the price and schedule for our classes, and Wit was extremely serious and polite. He's cute, I decided, but he's very, very young, and he's dull. Then he said, "I will take you home. I brought my motorcycle."

It was an unusually large road bike, and as I climbed behind him, he asked, "How fast do you want to go?"

"As fast as you can. I like speed."

Soon the neon lights of Rachada Road flashed by in an impressionistic blur, my bus map flew out of my book bag and disappeared, and I held my glasses in my hand because the rush of air threatened to blow them from my face. "Do you like this?" he turned to ask, and I laughed and nodded and wished the ride would go on for hours.

He proved to be a stern and demanding teacher, and I was tone deaf. He made charts and used hand signals to show how the sounds moved, but the noises that came from my mouth were flat. A million rules governed how the tones were made, and I floundered after the first three. It was humiliating and I took refuge in humor, American sarcasm, and was amazed when he would laugh. And after every class, he would take me back to my neighborhood on his motorcycle, zipping my heavy book bag under his jacket so the papers wouldn't blow away.

"Do you want to get something to eat before you go home?" he asked one evening as we reached the little street that led to my apartment.

"Yes. Would you like to come with me or do you need to go home?"

"It's up to you," he replied, and I said, "Please come."

There was a restaurant nearby that was almost empty, and a mosquito cloud of waiters hovered around us the minute we sat down. I asked Wit to order from the menu that I couldn't read, and internally reeled at the prices that were double those of much nicer places that I'd been to. The amount of food was double as well, a tub of soup, mountains of rice, and a mammoth platter of fiery shrimp and vegetables.

It was all delicious, but Wit was seething over the impossible portions and inflated prices. "They are taking advantage of you because you are farang. I don't know why Thai people do this; they think all farang are rich. You shouldn't come here again." He was embarrassed as well as outraged, so I told him several stories about greed and chicanery in the States and that cheered him up. The evening became very pleasant, with the food an incidental annoyance.

"I like that man," I told myself after he dropped me off at my door, "probably more than I should."

Our next class was a grueling one, over three hours of final consonants and tone changes. At one point, I sank to the floor in exhausted frustration and he sat beside me, saying, "Tell me one more time." The sexual tension was palpable, and I was unsure if it was all mine.

"Eddy, I have a problem," I said at lunch the next day.

"What is it?"

"I think my Thai teacher is cute."

"He is cute."

"Eddy, he's twenty-five."

"What? He's younger than me? He looks much older."

"Maybe he's lying about his age," I decided. "He acts older too. Maybe he's really thirty-five. That's not too young."

But he's not, I thought. He still has the anger and uncertainty of a twenty-five-year-old, and I could have easily been his mother.

Harold, a co-worker who was well into his thirties, had a new boyfriend who was nineteen. "You could be my father," the dear young man pointed out.

"You should have told him that if you were his father he would have been too well brought up to say that," I told Harold when I heard the story later. "I have a friend in the States who used to say if you could have given birth to it, forget it. Then she fell in love with a man who was twenty years younger and they're still together."

"Maybe she found out that age didn't matter," Harold said, and I stared at him, muttered "Hell," and changed the subject.

The Thai classes became longer, with extended cigarette breaks and conversations. Wit showed up one day with the front of his jacket zipped up and bulging. "Look, I'm pregnant," he grinned and then revealed a jasmine plant that was heavy with buds. "It will bloom at midnight," he said as he handed it to me, "and the sweetness is intense, because the flowers are still growing."

"Want to get food?" he would ask after class, and we went to noodle stalls with tables on the street where tiny lizards congregated on the dark walls nearby. "If you catch one and put him behind your ear, he won't be able to move. Do you want to try it?" he asked.

"Yes, please, I'd love it."

He jumped for one and caught it, but it scurried from his hand and out of reach. "I didn't want to squash it," he told me, and I began to love him.

"Oh, Eddy," I wailed the next day, "I'm too old to like Wit."

"No, you're not," he said. "Ask him to go to see *In Love and War* with you. It's a good movie; he falls in love with a nurse who's older than he is."

"I think I have to be more subtle than that, "I said.

"Doesn't he take you home after every class?"

"Yes, but only because he's very, very kind."

My struggle with Thai was challenging enough to keep extraneous thoughts out of the classroom but not my rebellious grumbles: "I hate King Ramkamhaeng; he made the Thai alphabet hard on purpose so farang would never be able to learn it," or "No. I believe in Santa Claus, I believe in the Easter Bunny, I even believe in some form of God, but I don't believe in an implied *hor heep*," a diabolical letter of the alphabet that can change a tone and is at times unwritten but still potent.

"I'm going to have a cigarette and scream," I told Wit after displaying exceptional stupidity for an hour.

"Don't," he said, looking apprehensive, but I went to the top of the stairs and uttered a muffled shriek. Eddy and his friends in the office below fell silent, and then one said "Janet" with an audible note of relief.

"I had to do it," I said as demurely as I could while trying not to laugh at Wit's look of horrified amusement. Yet I was gaining a slow glimmering understanding of how the language worked, and comprehensible words started to emerge from the incomprehensible street signs.

Then the baht plummeted from twenty-five to forty against the dollar, refugees streamed across the Thai border from the newly awakened battleground of Cambodia as Hun Sen toppled Prince Rannariddh from their shared Prime Ministry, and Wit told me about his girlfriend. Suddenly my world felt dangerously foggy and unstable. Moving closer to work seemed a good idea, since it would reduce the exhaustion and expense of commuting, and the amount of time that I spent with Wit after class. The move turned out to be expensive as well, what with deposits and first and last month's rent due at the outset. Money was tight and nobody knew where the economy was going, but it didn't look good.

"I think I won't be able to afford classes for a while," I told Wit. "I'm going to stop for a bit until things are better."

He grabbed both of my hands and said, "But I just want to teach you. If you were lazy or a bad student, I would worry about the money, but I'm a teacher, not a businessman. Pay me when you can."

But I was worried about him, watching him as he taught, pushing himself past the point of exhaustion, traveling on spirit and determination and gristle.

"If I'm being strange, it's because I have a headache," he told me at the end of class, and I could see the pain. "It's coming into my eyes. Do you know what I mean? I'm afraid I can't take you home tonight."

"Please don't worry about me. Go home and take care of yourself, "I said.

He stayed while I gathered my things and waited until I walked out toward the main road.

"Where are you going? Get on the motorcycle. I can take you as far as my neighborhood." As I settled in behind him, he said, "I heard a man ask you where you were going."

"He's the security guard. He's just doing his job, "I explained, and realized that the sooner I was in my new apartment and no longer Wit's responsibility, the better it would be for both of us.

"I've lost my brains," I said at our first afternoon class after the disorienting experience of transporting everything I owned to my new apartment.

"Then we can just chat," he said, looked closer at my face and asked, "Have you eaten?"

"Of course."

"What, bananas?"

"I'm not hungry," I insisted. "I ate this morning."

"Then let's go and have a Coke." As we walked to a noodle stall, he took my arm and I drew his hand close to my side, feeling absurdly happy. He bought food, we ate, and I thanked him as we finished.

"What should I say to you?" he asked.

"You're welcome."

"Is that all? Just 'you're welcome'? I want to say more."

"It's all right, you don't have to. I think I know."

"My friend," I thought, and struggled to hold that thought in place.

My new apartment was palatial by all of my former Bangkok standards, with a real living room, and a separate bedroom with a door, and a refrigerator, and a sizable balcony. It was far more comfortable than the classroom that we used and infinitely cooler, so we began to have our classes there in the afternoon. They often stretched to five hours, with nonstop conversations after agonizing battles with Thai.

He showed me how to put flint powder grated from a lighter on my cigarettes, making them flash like miniature sparklers. We argued about Thai behavior codes, with my painfully acquired conservative point of view clashing with his conviction that farang could do exactly what they pleased.

"Travelers maybe, but not if you live here," I protested. "I live here."

"Maybe," he replied sardonically.

We talked about a hotel fire in Pattaya, in which ninety people died because the fire escape doors had been locked.

"They didn't want people to leave without paying their bill. And after all, only ninety people died," he said in tones of disgust.

"Ninety people, and Thailand has sixty million."

"Exactly," he said and then muttered the farang mantra, "T.I.T." ("This is Thailand.")

"Don't say that."

"You know what it means?"

"Yes, and I hate it. But I have no right to talk. I'm not a tourist anymore, but I'm not a resident. I know I'll always be a guest."

That was the day that he gave me a hug and a quick kiss goodbye, and then held out his arm, where the hair was standing on end. I touched it, standing back, my own skin prickling. After he left, I called Rod, weeping, and he was with me in minutes.

"I have to stop this. I don't want to feel this way, but I'm in love with him," I sobbed.

"Did it ever occur to you that the feeling might just be reciprocal?" Rod asked.

"No, he has a life. He has a girlfriend. He doesn't need a woman in her forties. Dealing with my thought processes is hard enough."

So I drew away, he drew away, we worked ferociously on Thai. I struggled through translations, only to have him look at them and say, "This is very beautiful, but it has nothing to do with what the paragraph actually means," and point out the one mistranslated word that had thrown me off course. He gave me a children's story to decipher, a repulsive moral tale called *The Little Ant Mother*, about a baby witch whom I rapidly began to loathe. We avoided all that was personal until the day that we spent a long portion of the afternoon kissing.

"If we have sex, that will only last a little while, "I said. "If we're friends, we'll be friends forever."

Both of those statements turned out to be true. It's also true that no man has ever made me as happy as I was on the night when he asked, "May I kiss you now?" and when he held me afterwards, until I fell asleep.

8 ENVYING TRAVELERS

I was thoroughly in love, with Thailand, with Bangkok, and with Wit, in a tangled snare of emotion that made me high, happy, piercingly awake, and alive in a way that I'd never expected to be after entering my forties. I was a gleaming body mass of undiluted euphoria for weeks until the word *birthday* raised its ugly little head and sneered at me.

Age no longer seemed an important element in the equation that consisted of Wit and me and his girlfriend and our conflicting work schedules. My vast pool of ignorance had made him the guiding figure in our relationship; I went to him with my questions about language, culture and daily living, and he always had the answers. Then he turned twenty-six, and that event placed him inexorably and chronologically between my two sons.

I did my best to push that fact out of my mind, and I had plenty of farang examples to help me do it. One of my best friends in Seattle, Bill, had begun making semi-annual pilgrimages to Bangkok, where he invariably met a girl or two who completed his vacation experience, and who were often younger than his daughter. I went to parties frequently with Eddy where I watched his friends enchant vacationing Western men from all parts of the globe who were frequently twice the age of their Thai companions. If the generation gap didn't bother them, why should I care?

But I did care, and it did bother me. There was a built-in expiration date that came with this relationship and I knew it. If I truly loved this man, then I would want him to have the same experiences that I had already gone through—an equal partnership, having children, building a family. Not one of these things was going to happen for him with me, and that knowledge nagged at me in a little cluster of pain at the back of my neck.

I began to get ganja from Eddy and would retreat to my apartment by myself, to pack it into the shell of an emptied cigarette and inhale in a way that Bill Clinton never did, trying to erase the tension. It didn't work. As I smoked, I was caught in a cinematic loop of examining what I was doing with Wit, like the meditation on death that monks practice while looking at a corpse, accepting the inevitability of letting go, of accepting the end.

Music is often a generational benchmark, and so it was with us. One night when we were together I heard a song on the radio that I had listened to when my oldest son was a baby, when a young woman on the other side of the world was pregnant with the man I loved now.

"Remember when we talked about how if we were friends, we'd always be friends, but if we had sex that would only last for a little while?" I asked. "I think it's time for us to stop having sex and to work on being friends instead." And we did.

Stopping the affair was like losing one of my senses, and for a long time the world flattened out for me. I missed Wit, especially when he was with me, drinking coffee and chatting. He would smile and suddenly I'd remember seeing that brilliance in a dark room. It was a fragile time, and we were very careful to avoid any kind of touch.

One day, while we were redefining our friendship, I told Wit about a woman I'd encountered that morning while crossing a busy street. That was always an exciting experience in Bangkok, where pedestrians ignore traffic lights in favor of a slow process of gaining ground, like troops in a military exercise. A small break in traffic would permit an encroachment of several inches of road space, in which the pedestrian would stand while waiting for the next break in traffic. It was a thrilling and life-threatening passage that could take a lot of attention and a little time and it was best accomplished in a group.

Being a coward by nature, I liked to position myself in the middle of a cluster of street crossers, and on that particular morning found myself next to an elderly woman. She grabbed my arm, guided me through the nightmare of cars, asked me where I was going, and then led me to the closest bus stop.

"People like that make Bangkok special for me, and I want all foreigners to have that sort of experience while they're here," I told Wit.

His response was, "That's not for travelers."

As I thought about it, I realized that he was right. In the heavily tour-isted areas of the city, the attention that foreigners received was far more economically oriented than steeped in Thai culture. Off the beaten path of guidebook recommendations was where kindly attention and consideration were offered, in places where tourists had no reason to go. It was one of the benefits to being a resident, rather than someone who was passing through, and I usually was grateful that I received those hard-won advantages.

I told myself that I was learning how to live in Bangkok, that I was building a life there as carefully as I was working on my friendship with Wit. But sometimes I felt a stabbing envy of Bill, who came with his segment of vacation and his saved-up dollars, to have a good time with no need for soul-searching reflection. I saw female travelers lying bare-breasted on a beach, and I occasionally wished for their freedom. I knew I was greedy, but I wanted the privileges of both the resident and the tourist. True to my upbringing as an American woman, I wanted it all.

I was given an opportunity to try to have it all one night. I went to a party with Eddy where a young man with the eyes of a pirate assailed me with the immortal pickup line, "I like you. Don't you like I?" He was quite cute, but definitely younger than my youngest son, and when I pointed that out to him, he was honestly confused. "It doesn't matter," he assured me, as we both gazed into a room filled with men of my age who were quite happily paired with men of his age.

I was surrounded that evening by a community of people who wouldn't have flickered an eyelash if I'd left the party and gone to one of the city's hotels that catered to spur-of-the-moment adventures. Eddy would have laughed while quickly jamming some condoms into my purse as I walked out the door. There was nothing to stop me but the memory of the skin and the mind and the affection of my friend Wit, whom I still deeply loved.

"I do like you, but it does matter to me," I told him, removed his arm from my waist, walked back into the party and had a double Scotch. Yes, I decided, I do want it all. I want to be able to have good conversations before and after I have sex with men whom I truly like, I want to live in a way that allows me an untroubled night's sleep, and I want to enjoy all that is given, while accepting all that is taken away, by my decision to live in this city where my freedom was both expanded and truncated.

9 GHOSTS IN THE CITY OF ANGELS

Eddy's sister, Usa, is as sophisticated as she is miniscule. Well under ninety pounds, and less than sixty inches tall, even when wearing the three-inch, designer-knock-off heels that are her trademark, she is well-traveled, dresses like the world's shortest supermodel, and is capable of being dazzlingly caustic in two languages. She can cut through bureaucratic snarls at any Thai ministry you might care to name with the same charm that clears a path for her at a crowded Bangkok nightclub. Usa is smart and gorgeous, measuring at least 8.6 on the Richter scale, and she doesn't just think that there are ghosts in the world—she knows there are.

She's not alone. Ghosts are such an integral part of Bangkok that I'm sure they're included in the city's population count, and may well be the reason for that number's fluctuation. Eight million? Ten million? Who can be sure, when new ghosts enter the city with every house fire and traffic accident?

A generous portion of my bloodline is Irish, so of course I believe in ghosts, but they never became a fixture in my life until I moved to Bangkok. My introduction to the world of the spirits was benign, when I noticed a department store mannequin, a figure of a small boy, dressed in a shirt and short pants and standing at the edge of a lake. I was new in town and full of questions, and the answer to this little mystery was unsatisfying—"The motorcycle taxi drivers found a doll and they dressed it up."

My experience with motorcycle taxi drivers was limited at that point, but I'd watched them smoking, swigging Red Bull, and playing checkers with

Coke bottle caps, and they didn't seem like the kind of guys who would dress up dolls for fun. It wasn't until Halloween that I was given the answer in an issue of *Bangkok Metro* magazine. A woman and her son had died when their car plunged into the lake, and the little boy was seen at night standing beside the scene of the fatality, beckoning drivers toward the water, to keep him company. The mannequin was placed there to soothe the dead child's spirit, and to hold the gifts that were left for him.

I never made an offering to the ghost of the lonely boy, but I would silently greet him as I drove by. The idea of his spirit yearning for friends was a poignant one, and the day that I passed his statue and saw that it had been surrounded by soccer balls, I felt like crying. He had become real to me, and lived in my imagination, so I suppose, on a very low level, I had become haunted.

My adult students, each of them with at least one university degree, had their own personal ghost stories. Some were more than willing to tell them; others looked troubled and said, "I don't want to talk about it." This was clearly not the stuff that campfire entertainment was made of, as I learned when we moved into a site for our school, a vacant house that had a resident.

I never saw anything, but Usa and her friends didn't want to be there after dark, when water was heard running in the empty bathroom, and one of them saw a woman's legs passing by upstairs. Jessia, our housekeeper who feared nothing that drew breath, was quite vocal in her insistence that the ghost wanted us to leave. Our employer dismissed these stories, and one of the other teachers, who had lived in Bangkok for a while, issued a demand that none of this be talked about outside of our ranks. "It's all nonsense, of course," he said, "but if people think we're haunted, it will kill the business."

Then one day he brought his daughter, a bright little four-year-old girl, to work with him, because she wasn't feeling well. Sometime after lunch, Jem looked up at the empty staircase, and asked, "Daddy, who's that lady?"

"What lady, Jem? There's nobody there."

"Yes there is, that lady on the stairs. You know, the one who's smiling at me."

Jem was taken home, never to return, and the ban of silence was stricter than ever. Usa came to work one morning to find a pack of snapshots in the office that hadn't been there the night before, and we pored over them. They were from the sixties and the predominant figure in all of them was a woman, well-dressed in Jackie Kennedy fashion, with bouffant hair and an insouciant look about her. We couldn't ask about her in the neighborhood because we were forbidden to discuss any of this, and the photographs soon disappeared. Not long after that, everything went rapidly awry. The owner of the house broke the lease, claiming she needed it to turn into a restaurant, a business that never came to pass, and we found another spot for the school that had no supernatural undertones.

This is when I decided I wanted to move closer to work, and Eddy said he would help me find a place to live. We went to a building that had really nice apartments that were brand-new and, what with first and last month's rents plus a deposit, were almost out of my price range. I was juggling funds in my head, trying to decide how I could afford one of those delightful little one-bedrooms, when out of the blue, the owner of the building called Eddy and told him there was one apartment that was substantially less expensive than the others.

We went to look at it. Except for a few scuffs and scrapes, it was identical to the perfect ones that we'd seen earlier, and I closed the deal. There were a couple of days before I could move in that were paid for, so Eddy, a vacationing German friend of his, and Usa stayed there until I took possession.

We had a small housewarming gathering on my first night of occupancy, and Usa came to me looking worried.

"I think you shouldn't live here alone," she told me. "Maybe Lin and I should move in with you. There is a ghost here." Her reasoning was less than convincing, having to do with repeated knocks on the door late at night, with nobody visible when the door was opened.

"Someone was playing a joke on the new farang," I told her. "Don't be silly. This building hasn't been here long enough to have a ghost."

One morning I was in my bedroom getting dressed when I heard footsteps in my apartment and the closing of the bathroom door. This was a fairly normal occurrence because Eddy was a nocturnal animal who frequently danced until dawn in those accommodating clubs that refused to acknowledge the 2 a.m. closing time. My apartment was a convenient way station for a shower and a change of clothes before he went to work, so I'd given him a key, and often woke up to find him sleeping on my sofa.

I'll make some coffee; he probably needs it, I decided, and opened my bedroom door to find an empty bathroom with its door wide open, and a living room where I was the only person in it. Peculiar, I thought, chalked the whole thing up to some auditory version of a trick of the light, and forgot about it.

Then came the nights when I was awakened by the feeling that something was staring at me. This was a sensation that I was more than familiar with. Both of my children used to stand silently at my bed and look at me when they were small, because they knew it would wake me out of the soundest of sleeps, and my maternal instinct became so finely tuned to that feeling that I can be (and often have been) awakened by the gaze of a cat.

Perhaps this is why, when I would awake to see a form standing near me in the dark which made no demands for food or comfort or arbitration in some sibling skirmish, it was easy for me to roll over and go back to sleep. In the morning it seemed like some variant of a weird dream, and I always convinced myself that it was.

There was a shape that I almost saw clearly one Christmas night, when I woke to a sound so definite that I went into the living room, turned on the light, and saw an impressionistic outline of a body dissolve into my apartment door. This came at the end of a day when I'd been desperately homesick, had struggled not to cry when talking to members of my family in expensive trans-global phone conversations, and had met the girlfriend of the man with whom I was still in love. There were far too many things for me to feel as I struggled to sleep, and any supernatural visitor was simply an unwelcome intrusion. If I had any emotion to spare that night for what I was almost certain that I saw, it would have been expressed in an annoyed sputter of "How rude."

Several months later, Eddy, Usa, and their mother came over one evening. We were all happily relaxed and drinking beer when suddenly Eddy's mother stopped laughing, put down her beer, told Eddy that she had to leave, and said that we should all come with her because there was a ghost in my apartment. Eddy and I continued to drink our Heinekens, Usa obediently stood up to leave, and their mother took my hand in hers and peered earnestly into my face.

"Are you happy here, Janet?" she asked me, and when I assured her I was, she squeezed my hand, wished me good luck, and left.

"My mother is usually right about this kind of thing," Eddy told me, "Has anything bothered you? Have you been afraid?"

I told him about the vague hints of a presence that had made itself felt at random moments, and was surprised to see my usually skeptical friend look concerned.

"If it is a ghost, it's friendly," I assured him. "It's never frightened me or made me feel uneasy. There must be friendly ghosts, right? Look at Casper."

"Casper is not a real ghost," Eddy replied. "Don't forget they gave you a discount for this place. Be careful."

Then came the night that Wit came to visit with some Thai weed. I'd learned early on that smoking dope was, for me, not a good idea. The people I knew would empty the tobacco from Marlborough cigarettes and replace it with what they brought back from their slum runs. It was easy for me to smoke too much, when I held the familiar form of a cigarette and the illusory safety of a filter, and I never realized it until my mouth dried and I felt the drug hit my body with the force of an electric current.

But that night I was with somebody I loved and trusted, and everything was fine until I got up to get water for my suddenly parched mouth. My legs felt strangely light, almost floating, and something, somewhere, was calling me out onto the balcony. I had to grab the railing when I stepped out there, since my body lost all knowledge of gravity, and I knew I could float right over the edge.

Something, somewhere, was doing its best to tell me that I was okay, that all I had to do was to let go and fly. I tried hard not to listen, while wondering if I could let go of the railing long enough to go back into the security of four walls, and was grateful to feel Wit's hand on my shoulder.

He led me back inside and held me so I wouldn't float away. "Don't leave me," I said, "There's something here. There's something wrong." He stayed with me as the body weight drained back into my legs and whatever it was that had been calling me had gone away.

Was it a bad case of reefer madness, or a suicidal spirit yearning for company? The one person I told, Usa, was sure that it was someone who died there who wanted me to die too. I have no idea. I only know that in the six following months, until I moved into a house that looked haunted but wasn't, nothing stared me awake, I heard no noises, my balcony was a safe place once more, and I never again asked my classes to tell me their ghost stories.

10. SHOPPING 101

Unscented deodorant, unsweetened peanut butter, and baking soda tooth-paste all vanished from my life when I moved to Bangkok, where they simply didn't exist. That was a fleeting annoyance. What kept me awake at night were coffee beans, shoes, cotton underpants, and Indonesian clove cigarettes, which were all things that I had to learn how to buy.

Scooter taught me how to buy the cigarettes, although I never acted on the knowledge that he imparted. I would have had to go to the Indonesian Embassy and buy them from the guards there, which seemed too much like a drug deal and exactly the sort of thing that could revoke my work permit, so I smoked the more readily available Marlborough Lights instead.

The Thailand Tobacco Monopoly is a government institution and not some-thing to be toyed with. Its protectionism is so strong that once every brand of the wildly popular Philip Morris cigarettes disappeared from Bangkok for more than a month.

"Marlborough Lights? More Lights? No have," I was assured by shopkeep-ers all over the city. During that deprived time, I would use my commuting hours to scan store windows for the cigarettes I craved, and would retrace my route after work to snatch up whatever stock remained.

It was a battle. The Tobacco Monopoly had demanded a full list of cigarette ingredients, and Philip Morris, being no fools and well aware of the Thai tal-ent for replication, had refused to comply. So their cigarettes languished in an off shore container vessel until the right person was paid the right amount.

Then suddenly every pack of Marlboroughs in every color, the red that were too strong for me, the green menthol that ripped out my throat, and the silver that were just right, were in place once again on every street corner.

Indonesian tobacco interests didn't have that kind of placement because they didn't have that kind of clout. My friends would bring clove cigarettes back by the carton when they went below Thailand's southern borders, and then they would share. It was strange to have Jakarta cloves more exotic in Bangkok than American cigarettes (made in Malaysia), but that's globalization for you.

Rodney always had coffee beans, which he swore he bought at the neighborhood supermarket. I was sure he lied because I scoured the aisles of that damned place and only found stale and bitter ground coffee hermetically sealed in vacuum bags. Then one day I needed to have my shoes repaired, and there in the supermarket, far beyond the rows of food, where vending booths of all kinds competed for space, was the Tung Who corner, with five different kinds of beans and a coffee grinder.

I'd passed a large Tung Who store downtown as many times as I'd overlooked the Tung Who stall in the supermarket, and had dismissed it as a grim-looking Chinese grocery, with no idea that it was a place where coffee beans were roasted and sold. I quickly learned how to say, "I'd like 500 grams of coffee beans" in Thai, and my life became happier and much more energetic.

"She wants to know when you bought your underwear," Usa translated for Jessia, who stood nearby in my bedroom holding a pile of freshly laundered, faded underpants.

"In America, last year. I can't find cotton underpants here," I said mournfully. Underwear was for sale in every street market, but it was all slick and shiny polyester in gleaming colors. Department stores had their expensive counterparts in silk. Cotton ones, I decided, were "not beautiful" and thus unacceptable in Thailand, so I treasured the panties I'd brought from the States, even though Jessia's energetic hand scrubbing had rendered them all the same drab shade of off-gray and close to threadbare.

I came home the next day to an uncharacteristically beaming Jessia, who handed me a department store bag that held six pairs of sturdy all-cotton underpants. "Very cheap," she told me, as she refused my attempts to reimburse her. And they were, I discovered, when I searched them out for myself, tucked away in the sale bins of the lingerie department where I'd never bothered to look.

People who shriek against the curses of the globalized marketplace have no clue. I too hated the Boots Chemists that had sprouted up everywhere in Bangkok, as ubiquitous as McDonald's, until the afternoon that I was driven into one by a drenching rainstorm. By that time, I'd grown accustomed to the fragrance of Pantene shampoo, which was the least floral that I could find, and bought men's deodorant without shame for the same reason. I abandoned these imperfect solutions without a hint of regret after entering Boots—a place that mercifully understood scent, and sold coconut shampoo and grapefruit bath gel and bitter lemon deodorant. My bathroom began to smell like an orchard, and one of my housemates told me, "I know when you get up in the morning because I can smell grapefruit upstairs."

Conventional wisdom proclaimed that foreign women couldn't fit into Thai shoes, and that was cruel because cheap shoe stalls were everywhere. Five dollars would buy a plastic copy of shoes that CNN had shown on Paris runways the week before. The day that I risked public ridicule and learned that my size 7 1/2 feet were a gigantic but possible Thai size 38 was a moment of revelation that was almost Biblical. I threw away my over-repaired American leather shoes and began to wear gorgeous, unnatural, fashionable designer forgeries.

I kept a mental list called, "You know you've lived in Thailand too long when…" and wearing cheap Thai shoes was close to the top. They don't translate well when you return to the States. My silver cigarette-heeled sandals with bows at the toe-cleavage, which I bought for a Bangkok dinner party, have never touched the cement of a Seattle sidewalk. They sit in the back of my closet as a reminder of an alternate universe where shoes, like any other pleasure, last for only a little while, and shopping is a never-ending pastime, requiring skills that anybody, even a farang, is able to learn.

แลกชีวิต "SURVIVOR"

11. SURVIVOR

I would have run screaming from the dirty, dilapidated house that Rodney, Scooter, and I planned to move into in an attempt to join forces and conserve our devalued baht, if not for my dream of having an orange kitten. The place was, after all, on a soi called Red Cat, and our prospective landlord said we could have pets, so it seemed to be an achievable goal.

With a large amount of trepidation, I walked in for my initial surveillance of our new home, and was dazzled by the sight of a tiny orange feline, who arched his back and spat at me from the protection of a sliding glass door.

He was skinny and grubby and so were the three other kittens that lived in a little hole in the wall outside. The mother of them all was skeletal, fierce, and smart enough to know that she needed help and that I was the perfect dupe.

I called her Millicent the Malevolent and courted her with grilled fish and chicken. Soon she stopped snarling at my approach and began to accept worshipful attention after meals, while the kittens ventured out from their little cavern and tore ferociously at the scraps that Millicent had left for them.

This was a daily ritual, and Millicent shrieked with imperious annoyance when I was late. She sprawled near me one afternoon, with the kittens cleaning up the remains of her meal, when a large, villainous-looking orange male stalked into the courtyard. Ignoring my attempts at chasing him away, he sat at a distance assessing the situation. He came to sit on the wall above Millicent, watching my hand stroke her fur, then bent down, bit her on the neck, and took her place when she jumped away. As I tentatively touched his scruffy, dusty coat, I could feel a rusty purr under my fingers, and that's all it took for Dad to claim me.

He was a fearsome beast, with a large and permanent swelling on his left side and the ability to turn a chicken leg to small bone fragments in a matter of minutes. Rodney was horrified when he looked through the glass door one afternoon to find Dad on my lap, but by that time the orange kitten seemed appallingly dull compared to his feral father.

I was at work on the day that we officially moved into our new home so missed the scene of Millicent leaping with all claws bared onto the back of one of Rod's exuberant dogs. When I came home that night, the hole in the wall was empty and I was desolate. I went up to my room, heard a surly little grumble at the screen door, and there, out on what I assured myself would someday be a rooftop terrace, was Dad, grouchy and expectant.

I bought a bag of cat food, which he decided was edible, and Dad's nightly visits became a fixture. Walls made him nervous. Although my bed was a tempting novelty, after a few minutes of comfort he would stalk off into the night and join me the next morning for coffee out on the roof.

It was a melodramatic night of thunder, lightning, and horrendous rain when Dad screeched for me and strutted in with Millicent, who had been invisible for over a week. God knows how the kittens came up, but in the morning there they were, more savage, scrawny, and downright ugly than ever.

They were happy enough on the roof, until somehow they found their way inside and downstairs, where they defecated energetically on every available surface, before finding their way back up the staircase and outside. I cleaned up the mess with a toxic cleanser that seemed to be based on mustard gas, but Rod's dogs had caught the scent. They came bursting out on the roof to see where the party was, and Millicent disappeared with the kittens once more.

She returned with Dad for nightly meals and apparently had delusions of reclaiming her old turf because one evening there were two bleeding dogs and a small cat corpse that had been Millicent. That night there was a loud screeching at the screen door and Dad led me out onto the roof where there were two remaining kittens, one tabby that was cowering away from a tiny and very crazed replica of Millicent.

Remillicent, Rod called her, Godzillicent, I suggested, but no affection went with either name because that kitten was as savage as a *Velociraptor*. She would even spit horribly at Dad if food was involved and had the tabby kitten quite literally scared almost to death.

Having brought them to me, Dad seemed to feel that all parental obligations were filled and ignored his offspring during his nightly visits. I was leaving for the States soon for an extended family visit so I fed the kittens as though I were fattening Thanksgiving turkeys, hoping to bring them up to fighting weight before my departure.

Dad was rapidly taking over, since Jessia, a woman as stern as she was kind, had joined us to keep house, and the dogs were no longer allowed inside. He would stride into the living room when we were watching a video and lead me upstairs to the cat food, which led Jessia to regard me as an amusing lunatic. One night I came home to find Scooter hand feeding Dad morsels from his plate, remonstrating, "But he's hungry." That was when I began to understand that Dad was taking over the household, and while I was away, I had no fears for him.

During my time in the States, Rod assured me that he was holding Dad hostage to ensure my return. Yet when I was picked up at the airport to come home, Rod announced, "We haven't seen much of Dad for a while." I was much too tired and jet-lagged to react to his words.

But I was on the rooftop in seconds when Jessia said, "The cat's coming," several minutes after I'd walked into the house.

Dad followed me downstairs yowling for food, somebody went out to buy chicken, and I went happily to bed after he was satisfied, knowing my world was still intact.

Intact it was, but not unchanged. There were of course no kittens, although a mirror image of the original Millicent roamed the soi, as skeletal and wild-eyed as the *Velociraptor* kitten had been. A younger version of Dad was frequently seen lurking in the yard, and Dad himself seemed smaller and diminished, although everyone assured me that he was still the same size.

Jessia was the one who fed him now, and Dad looked for me only when he had a new wound to display. The lady at the corner pharmacy began to ask, "For you or for the cat?" because my only purchases from her were Tiger Balm for me or antibiotic ointment for Dad's frequently bloody ears.

While I was gone, other people had moved into what had been my old room in Rod's house, and neither Dad nor I found any of the four empty bedrooms acceptable substitutes. We tried. I redecorated one ground floor room with a red bedstead, mosquito net, masses of floor cushions, and a bowl of carnivorous fish, but it flooded in the rainy season, and I moved to an apartment. It was nearby, so I still came with daily food offerings, and Dad usually turned up to accept them.

I introduced him to Arun, carrying him as though he were the baby kitten I could sometimes convince myself that he was. Arun was far from convinced and turned as white as it's possible for a Thai man to become.

"My God, Janet, he probably carries rabies."

"It's all right," I said. "Millicent confused my finger for a piece of chicken once, and if I didn't get rabies from her, I never will."

"You can carry it if you've been in contact with it. Never, ever bite me." And I assured him I never, ever would.

The conversation stayed with me and resurfaced in my memory on the bright and lovely morning that Dad lay near my feet and the phone rang. I jumped up to get it and felt a quick sharp pain in my bare foot, and cat fur under my sole. We were both surprised, and Dad accepted my apologies before we examined the trio of little scarlet beads above my instep. He seemed to feel it was marginal compared to the large crusts of dried blood that usually covered his ears, and I was grateful because I'd seen all too often what Dad could do to a chicken leg.

I doused my foot with rubbing alcohol and read Lonely Planet's dire pronouncements on rabies. "What do they know?" I scoffed. "Look at all they say about people being drugged and robbed on trains, and that never happens." But an Australian at work had once been a veterinary's assistant, and he told me, "You have forty-eight hours to get injections."

My doctor was quite amused by the story and never looked at the bite, since it was after all on my foot. He agreed that injections were a good idea. "Or we can test the cat for rabies," and he made a chopping gesture near his throat.

Parting with fifty dollars was the easy part; the dreams that followed the injections were not. I would wake up sobbing after nightmares that were heavily influenced by Lucien Freud's paintings, and would stare into the dark for hours, sleepless and vacant. But the shots were painless, no longer injected into the stomach, and Dad's scarred little head didn't stare at me from a platter, so it was worth it.

"He didn't come today," Jessia told me a month later, but I could hear him meowing. When I called, he emerged from a storage area in the kitchen, moving slowly on three legs with a front paw dangling uselessly. His leg was almost severed and I had to force myself to look at it when he crawled up on my lap.

"I can see bone," Rod said, when he looked. "He's not going to make it."

"If you take him to the vet, all that will happen is that his leg will be chopped off," Scooter informed me.

I tried to bandage his leg with a clean cloth and antibiotic cream, but he tore the dressing off. The only thing I could do was to give him water cupped in my hands and scraps of chicken that I tore into tiny pieces. We sat together for hours on the kitchen floor and he stared at me as I whispered, "You're a tough boy; you aren't going to die," to his limp little body that seemed smaller every day.

But he ate more and more, and one morning when I was sobbing because he wasn't there and I knew he'd gone away to die, Scooter told me he'd seen Dad much earlier hobbling down the soi. He returned that night, triumphantly washing his dirt-covered, destroyed leg, and looked quite proud when it eventually fell off.

Maybe it stayed with him as a phantom limb, because Dad never realized how ridiculous he looked. One afternoon I saw a female cat running desperately down the soi, leaping onto the top of a concrete wall. Padding purposefully behind her was Dad, gimpy but lustful on his last legs. His jumping days were over, and when he saw her out of reach, he turned to me and screeched for help. I scooped him up and carried him into the house for chicken, where Jessia and I watched him eat, shaking our heads over the indomitability, and the inevitable fate, of our boy Dad.

12 SUVAPORN'S DAUGHTER

She was not a pretty little girl, which made her unusual in a country that was full of pretty little girls. She was gracelessly thin and sullen and grubby, and there was no reason why I should ever have become close to her.

She lived in a house behind a covered yard, where her mother sold rice and noodle dishes, and her father drank, a lot. He also raised toy poodles that came thundering out to greet anybody who stopped there to buy food.

I'd never liked poodles, but it was oddly charming to be assaulted by a horde of them while having lunch. They were remarkably clean and insistently sociable, two qualities that were definitely not shared by many other dogs in the neighborhood, and they won me over.

Equally friendly was their owner, Khun Suvaporn, a tall, skinny, charming drunk, who had a small but confident supply of English and a perpetual beer in one hand. He was handsome, in spite of a few missing teeth, and looked much younger than his taciturn wife, who spent her time at the shop entrance, facing the road, smiling without conviction, and cooking.

Two little boys, who were Suvaporn's grandchildren, lived there, and I soon fell in love with them. They were very young, with pale skin, light brown hair and wild curiosity. The four-year-old immediately learned that I spoke Thai about as well as his two-year-old brother, and that I carried an inexhaustible supply of Hall's lozenges that are sold as candy at every corner store, so we became friends. He would earnestly tell me which poodles were bad, how they had bitten him, and how much it had hurt, while his baby brother sidled up to us, poked me in the back, and shrieked when I would try to catch him.

"Teach my babies English," Suvaporn asked, and I brought them picture books, but the youngest carried his off to a safe distance and my boy, Neut, told me all about *Star Wars*, in Thai.

A thin, impassive, untidy young girl was there in the afternoons, after school. She played with the boys, while watching me warily, and Suvaporn introduced her as his daughter, Kik. "Please teach her English," he asked, "I am a poor man and the government school doesn't teach her to speak." Kik and I looked at each other with a shared lack of interest, and she went on playing with Neut and his little brother.

Suvaporn may have been a poor man, but he certainly was well supplied with alcohol. On my way to work in the morning, I would see him having breakfast with a huge jug of red wine on the table, and when I returned in the evening, he'd lurch welcomingly toward me with a beer bottle welded to his hand. In the afternoon, he was at a coherent and affable stage of drunkenness, and on my days off, that was when I'd have food, play with the poodles, chat with Neut, and try to make his little brother believe that I was really a very nice person, once you got to know me.

It was on one of my leisurely days, a cloudy, cool, December Sunday, and I was on my way to Lumpini Park to hear the Bangkok Symphony Orchestra give an outdoor concert. It was one of my favorite things to do, and I was happy when I stopped in for food at Suvaporn's. His wife was vigorously washing dishes with her back turned when I asked for fried noodles. Suvaporn and Kik both left the table with quick greetings as I approached, and then disappeared into the house.

The wife had large bruises on her arms and a stunning black eye. It was the first sign of violence that I had seen in Bangkok. My stomach tightened and I was unable to swallow the food that she carried to me.

"The little boys have gone away," she told me as I left, but they weren't the ones I had on my mind. Kik was who I thought of, as I watched clean and cared for children playing in the park. The sun was falling behind the city's skyline, turning the lake into brilliantly colored watered silk, the sweetness of light classical music filled the evening air, and I miserably realized, with a horrible intuitive recognition, that Suvaporn's daughter was a child whom he abused.

Rod cautioned me not to get involved, and my businessman student, whom I respected, said that helping without interfering was the right thing to do. I remembered the girl I had been when I was Kik's age, when my father had become a threatening and violent stranger, and had trouble sleeping at night.

"I will teach you English," I told Kik the next time I saw her on the soi, "every Sunday at three." Her face was transformed with the first smile she had ever given me as she repeated the time, but I had to walk down to bring her to class on our first Sunday.

"May my friend learn too?" she asked, and other teachers warned me, "You'll end up teaching the whole neighborhood for free."

But with the devaluation of the baht, Thailand had become an economic bloodbath and Suvaporn wasn't the only one who was poor. My world had shrunk to the size of my neighborhood; there was no longer money for adventures. I could barely afford the two books I'd bought for Kik and her friend, and, smiling, I refused every child who begged for lessons as I walked down the street.

After that first Sunday, Kik was always on time, scrubbed and gleaming and carefully dressed. Her eagerness broke my heart, and her emerging personality humbled me with the trust that was given with it. After a month, it was impossible for me to remember the girl I'd first met and overlooked.

She worked so hard at pronunciation, at relearning sounds that she had been improperly taught at school. She revealed a distinct flair for drama in classroom games, as a gifted comedic mimic. She showed me her rock collection, gathered on infrequent trips to the coast, and I begged a friend to bring her polished rose quartz and Tiger's Eye and agates when he came to Bangkok on vacation. She gently trickled water down my neck at the Thai New Year, Songkran, and berated a little boy who hurled his water at me in modern Bangkok style. She sparkled with confidence and seemed to have achieved the safety that comes with being notable within a community. People on the street looked differently at Kik, now that she received lessons that none of them could afford.

I went to the States to reconnect with my family, and when I returned a year later, Suvaporn had built a little bar on the street beside the noodle shop. He still assured me that he was a poor man, but his wife smiled frequently with no visible contusions, and Kik had a new bicycle. We made a stab at reestablishing our class, but she was enjoying the end of her childhood and the English lessons faded away. I saw her often, playing with friends on the street, helping her mother in the kitchen, shopping with other girls in the neighborhood market. She was still a little girl, flat and lanky and goofy and happy. I worried about her at times, when I passed Suvaporn's tables at night and the little counter festooned with colored lights with its small knot of ebullient drinkers. But I learned that our housekeeper, Jessia, and other women on the street knew Kik and watched out for her, and would probably severely damage any man who hurt her. "*Nong* Kik," Jessia called her, "Little Sister Kik," and I knew she was becoming part of the community of strong women who dominated our neighborhood.

Every soi in Bangkok is its own little world, and those worlds do not often mingle. When I moved a short distance away from Kik and her family, I seldom saw her. Then my time in Thailand was finally over, and as I was preparing to leave, Jessia told me that Suvaporn was dead.

It was a horrible death. He put his head in a dangling noose one drunken night. Kik saw and thought it was a game, until he kicked the chair away and his legs swung free.

I saw her soon after, racing past on her bicycle, her face closed up like a knife. She was alone, and her speed didn't slacken as she passed me.

On my last day, I took my camera and rolls of film and some money and went to the noodle shop. As I walked, I remembered Suvaporn telling me once that he was sick and the doctors couldn't help him. I remembered how he sent huge, heaping plates of food with Kik when she came to class during a time when there was little money for food, how he refused my attempts at payment, and how he looked as he said, "I will always feed you." Kik was standing at the entrance to her mother's food stall, and as I approached I could hear her father saying, as he had so often in life, "I give her to you. Take her with you to America."

I grabbed both of her hands and put my camera, film, and baht into them. "Listen to me," I told her, as she stared at me without response. "Take pictures of everything you see. Use the money at the Kodak store to develop them. Look, and take pictures. Someday I'll come back and ask you to show them to me."

Someday I'll go back, and she won't be there. A girl with Kik's energy and talent won't be making noodles and babies on a backwater street on the outskirts of Bangkok. One of the women will know where she is, and will tell me, and I can only hope that it will be a place where she will want me to find her.

13 FOOD FOR EVERY MOOD

On leisurely mornings, I ate *khao tom*—steaming hot chicken soup with rice, sprinkled generously with fried minced garlic. Paired with a glass of *oliang*, that strong, sweet, black, iced coffee, it was comforting and satisfying. Thai men usually eat this at the end of a long and liquid evening, but I liked it as a contemplative start to the day.

Usually, I moved too rapidly for breakfast and stopped only when blood sugar levels plummeted to absolute zero. This was the time for food that yelled, "Back into the trenches, soldier," and I looked for *sen yai pat kee mao*, fat and chewy noodles, fried with bits of chicken and lots of fiery little chopped chilies, or *khao moo daeng*, red pork with rice, along with some fresh orange juice that's bittersweet with the tang of salt. This was fast food of the best kind—delicious, restorative, and designed to send those who enjoyed it straight back to work.

At night when exhaustion had won the battle and I was barely able to totter home, *khao kaa moo* was my drug of choice. This soothing, artery-clogging meal guaranteed a stupefied sleep. Slices of pork leg edged with fatty skin were put with rice into a Styrofoam box and handed to me with a plastic baggie filled with the dark brown broth that the meat was cooked in. I helped myself to the whole chilies and raw garlic cloves that are eaten with this and found the strength to hurry to my apartment before it cooled.

On those lovely evenings when I had energy to spare, I found friends who felt the same. We walked back down to the beginning of our soi where darkness and moonlight turned the dirty canal into navy blue velvet flecked with gold. We balanced ourselves on precarious chairs that were coupled with restless tables on the side of the soi, which was also the bank of the canal, and ate *hoy taud*, an egg pancake that's studded with mussels and eaten with bamboo sprouts and banana blossoms. We drank *nam manao*, sweet and sour lime juice that was blended with enough ice to permanently freeze our sinuses, taking care that the glasses didn't slide off the table and roll into the water. From our instant sidewalk café, at our instant party, we talked and watched the soi, which at night was transformed into an open-air food bazaar.

At the end of the month, when everyone in Bangkok receives a thirty-day lump sum salary, it was time for lots of cold beer in the company of friends. We went to the garden of Hua Pree, our favorite restaurant, and filled the table with plates of food that we all loved best. We shared tender circlets of squid fried with garlic, a huge folded omelet stuffed with pork and vegetables, chicken fried with cashews and chilies, green curry with chicken and pea-sized eggplants that are globes of bitterness in the sweet richness of the coconut milk. The perfect beer food was a coarsely chopped mixture of pork and tomato and chilies, guaranteed to send flames from our ears until cooled with some of the accompanying raw vegetables and several gulps of frigid Kloster.

I came from a place where I had been taught that at times it's simply too hot to eat. In this new world of perpetual heat, there were days when my stomach went on strike. I found that a small bag of freshly fried bananas, eaten in the relative coolness of the early morning, would provide a satiety that lasted almost all day, and that a milkshake from one of the omnipresent Dairy Queens provided sustaining, though infantile, comfort.

As a transplant, I occasionally felt dizzyingly rootless in a culture that ordinarily entranced me. In a country that was foreign to me, I was the foreigner, the two-headed elephant who was always out of step.

On those off-balance days, I would seek out transplanted food whose roots have sunk so deeply that they are now Thai. *Poffertje*, the little Dutch pancakes, are *khanom krok*, cooked in dimpled iron pans on food carts—circular, crisp and filled with molten coconut cream and chives or corn. Madeleines are harder to find but worth the quest. When a street vendor lifts them from their scallop-shaped pans, they're so warm and fragrant, so much of a surprise that they would make Proust weep and write a whole new set of volumes about Bangkok. I also found deep solace in the restaurants on Chakraphet Road, near the Sikh temple, that have fed Bangkok's Indian community the food of their homeland for more than a hundred years.

On days when I was confined to the office, buried in paper, food came to me. The *kluay chai* man, with baskets on opposite ends of a pole that he balanced on his shoulder, cried out his wares in a melodious, rhythmical call that haunted me long after I left Thailand, paired with the memory of his pale, delicious steamed buns that are crammed with a green vegetable that tastes like a kinder, gentler relative of horseradish. The insistent tapping of two sticks heralded the approach of the noodle soup lady, whose cart included spoons and bowls that I would leave outside my doorstep after I'd finished eating, for her to pick up when she came back down the soi. The maddening, repetitive melody of the motorized ice cream cart drove me to furious, impotent curses each day at three, when it woke up every dog on the soi and sent them into a frenzied chorus of howls and barking. If I was lucky, that would be followed by the coconut ice cream man who rode a bicycle that held two metal freezer containers which in some magical way remained cold. He filled a paper cup with little scoops that were sweet and flavorful and a better mood elevator than Prozac.

Like seasickness, the loneliness and misery that came from living far from my family would strike without warning. Once, when I was immersed in this gloom, a food vendor in my neighborhood called to me, beckoning toward her cart that was laden with grilled chicken, a large covered basket, and a mortar and pestle. She chattered companionably as she made *som tam*, the green papaya salad that is the Northeast's gift to the rest of Thailand, asking me if I wanted it with lots of chilies and crab. She urged me to choose the piece of chicken that I thought looked most enticing, and dug enough sticky rice from her basket to feed me for days. She mashed dried chilies with fish sauce and lime juice into a dark, blood-like liquid, and smiled, knowing that I had been as warmed by her friendliness as I would soon be by her food.

Then I fell in love with a Bangkok man who brought me a pot of flowering jasmine that would release its scent at night, and took me to eat ice cream sandwiches, Thai style. He was delighted by my childish, horrified glee as I watched the vendor split a squishy, white roll of bread, add scoops of coconut ice cream, top them with a sugar syrup in which swam little balls of what looked and tasted like tapioca, and cover the whole thing with a drizzle of sweetened condensed milk. The soft bread absorbed most of the melting mixture, but some of it ran down my fingers. I walked with the man I loved, feeling sticky and silly and happy.

We took food home where he showed me how to make *miang kam* by forming a tiny cup from a leaf and filling it with dried shrimp, coconut flakes, minced ginger and shallots and lime and peanuts and chilies, topping it with a dark, sweet sauce. Later he taught me the way to peel *somo* and we ate segments of this papery, juicy version of grapefruit as we sat outside on the balcony. The sky darkened to violet, the light was golden, and together we looked at the deepening colors of the evening as we waited for the jasmine to bloom.

BEAUTY

14. THREE SEASONS

Thailand is a country where there is no autumn. Its endless cycle of bud, blossom, and a rapid fade is unprefaced by the brilliant colors of fall. Flowers are either in bloom or they carpet the ground, and hundreds of others burst into perfect replacements.

The sense of beauty here is agrarian. Buds imply promise and receive attentive scrutiny; fruitfulness is honored; that which has faded is useless and ignored.

More than one Thai man has told me that women are most beautiful at fourteen. It takes an acute eye to recognize this when pubescent girls are swaddled in loose-cut sailor blouses that whisk bosoms and waists into invisibility. Hips are covered in boxy, bulky navy blue pleats, and hair is chopped into bobs that are no longer than mid-jaw. Clumpy shoes and thick white socks obliterate their ankles. These are girls who have been slip-covered.

During their summer vacations, it's easy to see why. Freed from school regulations, the girls let their hair grow to their shoulders, they tuck their T-shirts into their tight jeans, and they are slender and gleaming and delectable.

They grow into the right to have waists in high school, happily abandoning the sailor blouses, and they tie their hair back with white-ribboned bows into swooping ponytails. They gain university status in demure white blouses and black skirts that are so tight and narrow that the girls who wear them walk as though they had recently undergone foot-binding. They are impossibly slender and slight, they murmur when spoken to, and few of them will allow their boyfriends to hold their hands in public.

Most of them are beautiful. They are all obsessed with beauty. One of my friends once was bitterly disappointed with a set of engagement photos because in one of the pictures her hands were posed in a way that wasn't beautiful. There is a beautiful way to walk, to gesture, to gaze out of windows. Features are endlessly and ruthlessly studied for imperfections, and on the morning of university graduation, girls are awake at 4 a.m. to have professional make-up artists spend hours applying cosmetics to faces that are beautiful when bare.

They get jobs, and become relentlessly fashionable, aware of a new style the minute that it erupts in Paris and tracking it down in the street markets where copies can be immediately found. Passionate about designer name brands, they are rarely elegant, after having lived most of their lives in school uniforms, but they are always trendy and very lovely.

They are still girls. They attach Hello Kitty accessories to their Prada knockoff handbags. They hold their hair back with teddy-bear barrettes and carry papers in plastic cases that are emblazoned with the icons of Sesame Street. They have special softened baby voices that they use for their boyfriends, and they pride themselves on being unable to go anywhere alone. They wear pink and ruffles and cartoon characters on their tiny pastel T-shirts. They are soft and sweet, like small tinted marshmallows, and Irving Berlin must have had them in mind when he wrote his hit song from the 1950s, "The Girl that I Marry."

Married, they become mothers, and drape themselves in huge parachutes of material that envelop their pregnant bodies. They turn into women and gradually they let their beauty go, with such finality that it must be with relief. They are impeccable matrons, well-kempt and without the slightest trace of style. They dress in joyless pastel suits made of economical fabric, and their hair is styled in a way that no breeze could ever ruffle. Eventually they resemble little walking bricks, and they look comfortably happy.

It's unusual to see a Thai girl who isn't beautiful, and it's rare to see a woman over forty who is. Ripeness is all, and then it's gone. What replaces it is power.

Aging women officiate at ceremonies, with an authority that has emerged with their years. Squat, sagging women extinguish clusters of flaming candles by putting them in their mouths. They sing in clear, confident voices, and as they wave scarves that are far brighter than any they would have worn when young, their thickened bodies dance without self-consciousness, claiming a hard-won place upon the earth.

Now in the States, as my waistline loses definition and my breasts succumb to gravity, as my stomach protrudes and my thighs thicken, I think of the diet regimens and the hair color that promise to transform me into a stringy, aging woman, with wrinkles increasingly pronounced by artificially brightened hair, and I shudder. I turn away from the chic black garments that once made my closet a Temple of Gloom, and I reach for blazing colors that will transform me into a gaily painted brick, dancing my way into old age, laughing and joking and singing with the beautiful old women of my other country, that place where summer's heat changes suddenly to the warmth of a cheerful winter.

TOILET

15. TOILET PAPER

Coming of age in the sixties, I learned to toss off scatological obscenities with the same casual aplomb that I'd show while enumerating ingredients for a recipe. I firmly believed that no word could shock me until I moved to Bangkok, where each time a student told me that he needed to leave class by announcing, "I toilet," I would reflexively twitch.

Americans cloak the elimination of body waste with a lexicon of sanitized and usually infantile phrases: bathroom, restroom, powder room, lavatory, little boy's/girl's room, the potty. The simple word "toilet" is avoided at all costs, a penchant for euphemism that is often carried to absurd extremes. A macho and adventurous guidebook for motorcycle travelers in Cambodia cautions its readers, "When traveling in isolated areas, don't leave the beaten path when you need to go to the bathroom." Pretty little images of color-coordinated tubs, towels, and toilets presided over by Martha Stewart, surrounded by acres of landmines and frequented by men who resemble Hell's Angels, instantly spring to mind.

Cambodia, I learned from books that I borrowed from the Neilson Hays Library, that wonderful expatriate oasis filled with books written in English, has historically been a country where toilet habits have been a source of discussion and consternation. Chou Ta-Kuan, a Chinese diplomat living in Angkor Wat at the end of the thirteenth century, was bemused by the Khmer attitude toward body waste.

"No fertilizing use is made of human dung, which they look on as an impure practice," Chou observed of the Khmer. "Chinese who travel to this country never mention the use of dung in China, for fear of rousing Cambodian scorn. Two or three families join together in digging a trench, which when it is full, they cover over and sow to grass, digging another one elsewhere. After visiting the privy, they always wash themselves, using only the left hand; the right hand is kept for use at meals. When they see a Chinese cleaning himself with paper at the privy, they jeer at him and indicate their unwillingness to have them enter their homes. Some of the women make water standing up—an utterly ridiculous practice."

His humiliation at the local disgust toward his personal hygiene is nicely balanced by his snide comment about Khmer female urination, and he follows that up with an insightful remark that continues to stun readers 900 years after it was written. "It is my humble opinion that leprosy results if one takes a bath immediately after sexual intercourse—a practice which, I am told, is very prevalent here," Chou observes, thus placing Khmer standards of cleanliness at the forefront of medieval civilization worldwide.

His statements echo through the centuries with present-day travelers in Asia reacting with his same discomfit and disgust. China, with praiseworthy pragmatism, has addressed the primary Western qualm by installing sit-down toilets of gleaming sterility in Beijing, while continuing to suppress the followers of Falun Gong.

Western toilets abound in Bangkok, although the stalls all too often come without a supply of toilet paper. Toilet paper by the roll is available for free as napkins at any noodle stall, but is doled out in pathetic scraps for two baht apiece from vending machines, or is sold by attendants in public toilets.

Reiterating the ancient Khmer conviction that it's not possible to clean the buttocks with paper, most toilets in Thailand are equipped with a spray hose. This refinement effectively delivers the elusive "shower to shower" freshness promised by Western potions and powders at the tiniest fraction of their cost.

The ecological implications of a toilet that functions without a need for cases of accompanying tissue are obvious, and can only be viewed with repugnance by cultures that are so notoriously casual about hand washing that written instructions on elementary hygiene, complete with diagrams, can be found posted in every public toilet.

Many Westerners find that Asian squat toilets tone the thighs as efficiently as any Stairmaster does, with the added benefit of discouraging the formation of hemorrhoids. This could well be the reason that they've never caught on in countries that depend on the successful sales of hemorrhoid ointments, exercise machines, and feminine hygiene spray.

The American "bathroom" would be a revolting idea to traditional Thai homeowners, whose toilet is not only separate from the bathing area but is also completely detached from the main house. In these little toilet outbuildings, a vat of water is available for cleansing purposes, including a thorough soaping and scrubbing of the hands.

Separating the toilet from the bathing area has a logic well appreciated by anyone who has frantically danced in a panic-stricken jig while waiting for the end of someone else's lengthy ablutions. Domestic tranquility is preserved by allowing toilet and bathing functions to stand separate but equal, and may account for the close and tolerant affection commonly found in Thai households.

Like Chou Ta-Kuan in thirteenth-century Cambodia, many modern travelers throughout Southeast Asia are startled by the region's toilets and the accompanying questions presented about different cultural norms of cleanliness. Some of us return to our home countries, yearning for a simple porcelain bowl fitted into the floor, a spray bidet hose, and the freedom to ask, "Where is the toilet?" when we have no intention taking a bath, a rest, or a powder.

16 ESCAPES FROM BANGKOK

Two good things happened after the baht lost almost half of its value, shortly after my first full year in Thailand. It became very easy to stay thin, and almost everybody I knew became a citizen of an egalitarian society, since only a handful of people had any money. With salaries dribbled out in what was now a cruel joke, suddenly Usa, who worked in our office; Phibun, who was our motorcycle messenger; and I were all on the same poverty-stricken level, although Phibun, as a property owner, outranked both Usa and me—the motorcycle belonged to him.

Holidays were transformed into dismal wastelands of time, with no money to travel or go out on the town. Watching CNN and doing the crossword puzzle in *The Nation* were my recreational highlights, and I had a raging case of cabin fever by the time the New Year's break arrived. Somehow Rodney managed to come up with a thousand baht of additional salary for everybody, which amounted to about twenty-five dollars.

This was far more money than I'd had in my hand for a very long time, and a sane human being would have salted that away as survival funds. Since I was crazed from house arrest, I promptly bought a third class, hard-seat ticket for the night train to Nong Khai, in the far northeast where the Mekong River separates Thailand from Laos.

For less than two dollars, I was able to travel half the length of the Kingdom in discomfort that was not unbearable, and I spent the rest of my financial assets on tuk-tuk rides to and from the train station, a couple of meals, and a room in a riverside guesthouse. I watched every baht. I had become the quintessential cheap-ass foreigner that I'd always looked at with disdain, but it was worth it. For twenty-four hours, I escaped the claustrophobic comfort of my apartment and luxuriated in the quiet of an uncrowded little city, where I spent hours walking beside the Mekong. In the evening I sat on the guesthouse verandah, watching the four or five pairs of headlights that I could see across the river in Laos. In a weird way, I felt rested and ready to work and starve once more when I returned to Bangkok on a train that was packed with people occupying every available inch of space after the long holiday.

Back in the days when life had been fat and flush, holidays were spent on the island of Koh Samet, in a glut of sunlight and beer and food, sleeping in a hillside bungalow and feeling pampered. After my trip to Nong Khai, Samet felt like a giant adult playpen, safe, cozy, pretty, and not where I wanted to be. I never again journeyed with so little money, but from then on, when I had time to spare, I went as far northeast as I was able to go.

My favorite places receive scant praise from guidebooks, which was just fine with me because I'm not fond of sharing. I began to choose destinations based on the number of Khmer ruins that could be found there, and in the process became quite fond of Lopburi.

I fell in love with Lopburi at first sight, when I whisked past it at sunset on an express train from Chiang Mai and saw the mysterious remnants of the Cambodian Empire that had ruled there long before the Thai established their own kingdom. Standing stones enclosed by walls of rock were bathed in golden twilight. The sight of them took my breath away and was all that I needed to draw me back.

I read everything I could find about this city that had been eclipsed by the later glories of the Thai capital, Ayutthaya, and learned that its high point had been from the eleventh through thirteenth centuries, when it was under Khmer rule. It was now famous for its thriving population of monkeys, who were feted each year at their own banquet, an event that drew tourists from less simian-plagued corners of the Kingdom.

The train ride to get there from Bangkok is short and stops at every spot along the way, where people come rushing out to feed the travelers. The most wonderful coconut ice cream that I've ever eaten was sold to me through an open train window somewhere along the tracks to Lopburi, and I always made sure that I had an appetite before I began my trip.

The old part of Lopburi is a walking town, filled with enigmatic and time-worn pieces of its past, along with cheap hotels—an unbeatable combination for me. I loved to get there in the late afternoon and watch the sun set on Khmer structures so old that nobody really knows what their function was, or wander through the demolished portions of Phaulkon's Palace, the once-luxurious domicile of that ill-fated Greek adventurer who rose too high in the estimation of King Narai and was killed by jealous nobles.

The park that surrounds the Royal Palace once used by King Narai and later by King Mongkut is one of the quietest places that I've ever found in Thailand. Wandering through, I pictured lamps glowing in the little recesses that covered the sheltering walls, elephants carrying royalty and revolutionaries through gates that had been designed to accommodate pachyderm bulk, and French emissaries as dazzled by the spectacle of Siamese power as I was by imagining it.

Across the road from this former palace of kings is the Asia Lopburi Hotel, which is Spartan and ugly and friendly and usually clean, only steps away from a market filled with wonderful things to eat, and near a cheerful little restaurant called The White House Garden. These refuges made Lopburi my quick remedy for Bangkok burnout, close enough to reach on late Saturday afternoon and leave on Sunday evening, making it the ideal location for restless, cash-impaired teachers of English.

Although monkeys are more commonly seen than dogs on any street in Lopburi and are so dominant at Prang Sam Yot, a thirteenth-century temple, that the ticket taker is kept in a cage while the monkeys run amok, Petchaburi will live in my memory as the true monkey capital of Thailand. The hills behind the town are noted for a palace of King Rama

IV and a thriving, aggressive community of monkeys. Vendors sell bags of edibles that can be fed to the monkeys by sightseers who trudge up the slopes along a surprisingly arduous royal road, and the bag that I bought was empty in seconds. I carried it with me, looking for a litter barrel, and the monkeys became meaner and more menacing with every step I took.

I stopped and watched the other climbers, to see if they were being threatened as well, or if I bore some invisible mark of Cain that was visible only to simian eyes. Those who walked empty handed were left alone; only those of us who were stupid enough to buy monkey treats were under threat of assault, so I made my way to a garbage can and walked off in peace. Later I saw a monkey leap, gibbering and furious, up toward the face of a woman who carried a little bag of potato chips, and realized that the hills of Petchaburi were no place for a picnic.

The town was, however, a great place to relax. The Rabieng Rim Nam Guest House, an old wooden house on the banks of a little river, was hospitable and charming. Its multi-paged menu listed food that was better than that of any other hotel or guest house I'd ever stayed in, and it had an upstairs sitting room where I found a paperback mystery by Faye Kellerman and spent a happy evening reading and drinking beer.

There was, of course, my obligatory Khmer temple of Kamphaeng Laeng, and the giant Buddha shrine in the cave at Khao Luang, and shops that sold cheap and pretty sundresses, and a bus that took me to the beach at Cha-am with its fabulous fresh seafood and its dense forest of beach umbrellas that kept people properly pale. Best of all, to my frazzled Bangkok mind, was walking down the main streets of a town that still had more wood than cement, and where the traffic was not yet of homicidal proportions. Petchaburi was a splendid place to sit while blood pressure levels plunged to manageable levels and tension dissolved. It was like being engulfed by a giant alpha wave, soothing, somnambulistic, and very pleasant.

The place that I think of most often, and where I hope to live someday, is the northeastern town of Sisaket. After several years of Bangkok's relentless concrete gray, my eyes were ravenous for any shade of green, and Sisaket's grass and trees seemed almost blindingly and profusely emerald. The streets were dominated by pedicab drivers, who drifted by silently, eyebrows raised in question as they passed by me, grinning.

A gigantic food market with buckets of fermented fish sauce, whole pigs' heads, live fish whipping about in pails, frogs with legs bound together whooping hopelessly for freedom, and a huge hand-cranked machine that appeared to be extracting coconut milk, was my favorite place to wander, a bag of iced coffee firmly in my grip, among the crowd of early morning shoppers. A cluster of neighboring blacksmith shops where teams of men sledge-hammered hot iron into knives and farm tools gave the area a clanging rhythm that was synchronized and almost melodic.

Best of all were the street corners marked with skeins of pale yellow silk, piled waist high and looking like thread spun from durian. Women sat waiting beside stacks of neatly folded, gleaming fabric that caught the light, stopped me dead in my tracks, and stripped me of most of my disposable income.

Sisaket was the launching point for my favorite Khmer temple explorations, from the thin, blackened Buddhas of Prasat Kampaeng Noi to the sweeping magnificence of Prasat Khao Pra Viharn, but it's the people I met there who stay in my memory and make me long to return. "They are very sweet," a Bangkok refugee, who came, stayed, and owned a fabulous som tam stall, told me, and that was the truth. All of the people I met there—from the monk who patiently showed me how to make merit at a temple, to the women who helped me buy Thai country music in their little shop, to the bellboy in the Prom Phiman Hotel who sounded like an adolescent, Brandoesque Mafioso—were the kindest I have ever met in all of my travels. That, combined with thunderstorms that rival any man-made fireworks, and food that makes me want to sob when I think of it here in the United States, keeps Sisaket alive in my memory. "Go there," I tell my friends, "and then leave it alone. Sisaket belongs to me."

17 AMONG THE LIVING

When Cambodia crossed my mind, I immediately thought of death. My only nightmare before going to live in Thailand in 1995 had been about the Khmer Rouge, after an evening spent watching *The Killing Fields*. In Bangkok I soon learned from the newspapers that Pol Pot was still active, and the Khmer Rouge had strongholds near the Thai border. Photographs of a lavish, resort-like compound housing Ta Mok, "The Butcher," and his cohorts were featured in a glossy English-language magazine. Pailin, a gem-mining town in northwestern Cambodia, was off-limits to all but the Khmer Rouge. Given the kaleidoscopic volatility of Cambodian politics, it was hard to tell in the mid-nineties what power these killers would wield in the future.

I was afraid to go to Cambodia in the spring of 1997, but still wanted to without understanding why. When I stepped out into the night after landing at the Phnom Penh airport, my first glimpse of the place I feared was small children laughing as they played with luggage carts. A cluster of motorcycle drivers who were smoking in the shadows offered their services and backed away when I asked for time to have a cigarette of my own.

It was silent compared to the blast of constant noise that characterized Bangkok. Above the sound of the children and the low murmur of the drivers' voices, I could hear leaves rustling in the night breeze. There was a strange feeling of tranquility, and I was surprised that I felt safe.

I'd read about a guesthouse near the river called Bert's Books, owned by a former Alaskan who boasted "the only cerebral hostelry" in Phnom Penh. He sold used books as well as beds, with the slogan, "Always carry a book; you won't look so damned stupid." That was where I asked one of the motorcycle drivers to take me, and we putted down dark, wide streets, where little bonfires and candle-lit vending stalls were the only illumination. There was no traffic, very few people, and the motorcycle driver was solicitously cautious.

"It's okay. You can go fast. I'm from Bangkok," I told him.

"I like to go slow," he told me, and did.

It was amazing that he spoke English. I was used to Thai taxi drivers who routinely asked me, "Where you go?" and then found me incomprehensible in two languages. I had anticipated a lengthy tour of Phnom Penh before arriving at Bert's and was delighted when I was wrong.

"How much?" I asked, as we stopped at the guesthouse's open door.

"What you want to give," was his stunning response, and then, "What time tomorrow?"

"You will remember?" he asked, after we arranged a time.

"Yes," I replied, and didn't.

Bert's was shockingly bright and crowded and loud, after my peaceful journey into the city. The loudest and most comfortable looking man was big and bearded and had to be Bert.

"Do you have a bed for another Alaskan?" I asked.

"No more beds, but we can give you a hammock on the roof." He was interrupted by an agitated speech in Khmer. "Sorry," he said, "but some German's going crazy upstairs. Do you play Scrabble? Have a beer. I'll be back."

Clutching a can of Tiger beer, I turned to see the world's tiniest Scrabble board being set up an aging blonde with an East Coast accent and a profile straight out of a Cole Porter musical.

"I'm Lois. I just got in from Battambang," she informed me, and the room at large. "The head of the Tourism Bureau there came and told me to get back to Phnom Penh where I'd be safe. I'm a New Yorker, I know my way around, but this place is nothing like Central Park West."

"Who wants to play Scrabble?" she challenged. "I always win. I play in the Poconos every summer." Only one of us faced off against her, with the rest cowardly kibitzing from the sidelines. It was a spirited match, dissolving rapidly into mutual disgust.

"*Jain* is a proper noun," Lois sneered, and her opponent retreated to a permanent beer break when told, "*Ab* is a word. It's in the Official Scrabble Dictionary."

Bert returned, looking annoyed. "He's tearing his room apart. Call the police." His Khmer brother-in-law had a lengthy and animated telephone conversation, ending with the translation, "Maybe they'll come; maybe they won't."

"Janet, you can sleep in my bed tonight with my wife and kid. I'm going to have to stay near the German to be sure that he doesn't wreck the whole place. Of course the baby will probably pee all over you."

A beautiful Cambodian woman standing nearby said, "I'm Mrs. Bert. Come with me."

"You first," she said, pointing to a bathroom, and then tucked a mosquito net snugly around the bed that I collapsed upon after my shower.

I awoke in the night to the touch of the baby's hand on my arms, and the softness of his small and snuggling body. Loud, explosive sounds broke the stillness, but the baby moved gently in his sleep and Mrs. Bert never stirred.

Huge pots of good coffee and edible croissants made me rethink my position on colonialism the next morning. Lois had already packed up her Scrabble board and was ready to leave.

"My God, they were shooting at us last night," she shuddered. "I'm going to Vietnam."

Looking questioningly at Bert, I was relieved to see a grin beneath his beard. "Some soldiers drove by early this morning and fired a couple of shots in the air. Their party got a little out of hand, but there's nothing to worry about."

He turned back to his interrupted conversation. "I don't care if it's cheaper," he told some other departing travelers. "Those boats usually sink, they're so overloaded. If you're lucky, you'll only lose your cameras."

The room crackled with far more adrenaline and energy than I felt comfortable with before finishing my first cup of coffee. Looking for a quiet place to ease into the morning, I went up to the deserted balcony. The sweep of sky was breathtaking and two rivers converged a stone's throw from where I stood. Watching the Tonle Sap flow into the Mekong, I felt prickles of gooseflesh on my arms and tears in my eyes and muttered, "Oh, shit. I'm falling in love."

Mrs. Bert appeared, with assurances that a room would be waiting for me at the end of the day. "Get the key when you come home." Bert was waiting when I came downstairs. "Be back before dark. It's not good to be alone after sunset," and I had to restrain myself from replying, "Okay, Dad."

There was a motorcycle waiting outside and the broad smile under the baseball cap looked familiar, but when I'd finished depositing my visa forms at the Thai Embassy, I realized I'd made a mistake. There were now two motorcycle drivers waiting, one looking amused as the other said mournfully, "I came to get you, but you didn't remember."

Apologizing to both, I overpaid the man of mistaken identity and climbed onto the motorcycle of the night before. At a leisurely pace, we joined Phnom Penh's morning traffic, a sprinkling of pristine white Toyotas standing out among motorcycles and cyclos. "Hello" with a smile was apparently standard Khmer passing etiquette, since those who went by us did so with a wave, a greeting, and a friendly little tap on their horn.

The Thai Embassy was one of several beautiful, old French villas on a tree-canopied street, but bright, unshaded sunlight glared on the boulevard that we now traveled, and the only greenery to be seen were the vines cascading over walls that enclosed piles of rubble. Women crouched at the roadside with bamboo trays of food balanced on their heads, or stood near tiny mountains of carefully stacked baguettes.

Wat Phnom is where Phnom Penh began, according to legend, and so seemed to be the right place to begin exploring. It was a large hill in a wooded park, with steps leading up to grottos housing statues of the Buddha. It was also a place of shelter for tribes of little children, who followed me and ravenously accepted every dollar that I carried with me. A group of them escorted me back to the motorcycle and reached for my Marlborough Lights as I shakily tried to light one.

"Don't give them cigarettes," my driver said gently and started the engine.

The children retreated, except for one very little boy, who clung to the back of the motorcycle and stared at me until I led him back to the others. This encounter was disturbing, and would have been even more if I had known that before Pol Pot, Wat Phnom had been enclosed by an amusement park where children came to play and eat ice cream. "Children in Cambodia are very poor," my driver said, as he took me to the cool shelter of the Foreign Correspondents' Club.

I hated it on sight, an ersatz Casablanca setting for Bogart wannabes, but it gave me dollars in change for two Coca Colas to go, which was fortunate because I needed them for the amputees who waited outside the Royal Palace and the National Museum.

The splendor of the Palace was a cruel juxtaposition to what existed outside of its walls, but the National Museum was a storehouse of treasures that revealed the beauty of Cambodia's past. It contained figures of delicate loveliness, carved when Europeans were still painting themselves blue; statues that seemed to have torn their bodies free of the stone that had imprisoned them; and gods with transfixing power. "Shiva, the god of creation and destruction," I read beside one figure, and raised my eyes to see a Khmer face gazing from the sandstone.

It was late afternoon when my driver took me away from Phnom Penh down a long gravel road to his house and family. There were cows and chickens and fields and children who were loved and who attempted to teach me words in Khmer without success. The trip back was faster than usual, as we tried to match the speed of the setting sun. Riding in the lengthening twilight, I knew the excitement that makes people take risks, and I entered Bert's tightened with the adrenaline that I'd retreated from that morning.

"I was walking down Monivong Boulevard this afternoon," a young Australian told me as I gratefully fell into the cold beer that Bert had put in my hand. "A soldier holding a machine gun stopped me and asked, 'Where you come from?' I was shaking but I answered him as calmly as I could. 'Where you go?' he demanded, and I said I was taking a walk; was that a problem? 'No,' he said and he was smiling. 'I just want to speak English.'"

Browsing the shelves of used books that lined the walls, I asked Bert how he came up with his slogan. "It's from Alaska. I used to know an old guy in Anchorage who was functionally illiterate. Every morning he'd pass a little Native kid selling papers and every day he'd walk by without buying one. One day the kid grabbed him by the coat and said, "Hey mister, the paper's only a dime. Are you too cheap to buy one from me?"

"Leave me alone," the guy said. "I can't read, you little bastard."

"Well buy one anyway," the kid said. "If you carry a paper, you won't look so damn stupid."

James, the baby, was falling asleep in Bert's arms, and his wife was helping a traveler use the Internet. "I met her when I was here with the UN, working on the election. You should have seen her when we first opened this place. If a foreigner talked to her then, she'd run away and hide." He looked down at James and smiled. "This country's given me everything I ever wanted."

The next morning people waved and smiled and called hello as we drove down dirt paths toward the Killing Fields, Choeng Ek. Rice fields as flat and green as pool tables stretched toward an infinity of sky. Turning onto a long driveway, my driver stopped and said, "You go; I wait here."

The early sun drew moist smells from the bushes at the roadside. Bees were all that could be heard, and the air was still as I approached a tall monolith. Suddenly the air held weight, a dense and heavy barrier that I had to push through. Then the road ended. I was crunching on little, dry plants and rising before me was a glass-paned, wooden tower, filled with skulls.

The silence was absolute, the earth under my feet was barely alive, and the pits from which bodies had been excavated were very small and very shallow. I felt that it was impossible for anything to bring life back to this sacred and terrible place.

The faces that had once covered the skulls at Choeng Ek were waiting at the Tuol Sleng Museum, wall after wall of black and white photographs, documenting those who were killed there. Once a high school, it was turned into a torture center for those who were educated, and is now a memorial. "My parents were teachers," my driver told me when he left me at the entrance, "They died in this place."

That night I read in the *Phnom Penh Post* of the funeral for a young Khmer man who had died in Rwanda. A survivor of the Khmer Rouge camps, he had made his way to the States where he got a degree from Columbia. He returned to Cambodia, married, started a family, and then went to Rwanda with the UN because, he said, so many countries had helped his that he needed to give something back. Quoted as saying that the cruelty of Rwanda far surpassed that of Pol Pot, he was asked to stay in that country beyond his allotted time and was killed there.

On the day that I returned to Bangkok, I could barely move, paralyzed by my reluctance to leave Phnom Penh. I sat by the Mekong that morning, eating bitter little grilled bananas and feeling oddly homeless.

"I don't know where I want to go. Take me to the airport and I'll wait there," I told my driver.

"No, not yet. Your flight isn't until three," and he took me away from the city. We traveled across the river to a wat that was shaped like a boat and shaded by a bodhi tree; to another that he called the Brown Pagoda, where teenage monks followed me in disconcerting numbers, asking me to return and teach them English; and to his home where his brother said, "I want you to come back. I want to talk to you for a long time. Pol Pot killed my parents."

When finally we approached the airport, I thought about the man sitting in front of me on the motorcycle. He had become my friend—who had watched me cry at the Killing Fields and Tuol Sleng; had shown me where to buy a *krama*, the large iconic checked Cambodian scarf, saying, "Not that one. That's for tourists"; had taken me, unasked, to a place where it could be hemmed; had made me order food when I gulped a beer after touching blood stains on the floor at Tuol Sleng; had given me his baby to hold in my arms; had tapped a large burlap bag at his house and said, "Rice. We eat it every day."

He paid to have his little boys go to school. They were children who played football with an old shoe; the only book that they had at home was a discarded airlines timetable written in English, Japanese, and Khmer, and they gleamed with the love that their parents gave them.

I got in line to board the plane to Bangkok, covered with a fine film of Khmer dust, which I longed to have seep into my skin in the same way that Phnom Penh had entered my heart. Saying goodbye was impossible, without promising myself, and praying, to come back.

18 TODAY, WHERE DO YOU GO?

Waiting for daybreak in a filthy hotel room with blood smeared walls and a bed full of ravenous insects, I reminded myself that this was only happening because I was chasing a dream. For years I had wanted to go to Khao Pra Viharn, the disputed mountain temple on the Thai-Cambodian border that had belonged alternately to each country until the World Court ceded it to the Khmer people in 1962. Older than Angkor Wat, dating from the ninth century, it had been one of the last strongholds of Pol Pot and a frequent battleground until his death in the late 1990s. The only way to reach it at the beginning of the twenty-first century was by arriving from the Thai side, and the easiest way to do that was to take the train from Bangkok to Si Saket. This is why I was now miserably slapping at mosquitoes, listening to shouts and laughter from the bus station across the street, in a room that conjured up visions of Sid Vicious' final days.

A large hotel that was festooned with enough lights to illuminate every Christmas tree in the continental United States had beckoned as the train wheezed into town, but I'd wanted character, not comfort, and had gone to the Hotel Si Saket instead. As I curled up on the plastic loveseat and stared at holes in the window screens, I wondered if Si Saket was a breeding ground for malarial mosquitoes, and whether I'd lose my work permit if I went into Cambodia without a re-entry form to present when I came back into Thailand.

My boss had warned me that my visa and work permit would be invalidated if I didn't get a re-entry form, but our secretary had called

Immigration and assured me that I didn't need one. Everyone I knew had a different opinion, so I climbed on the train, hoping I had enough cash for an acceptable bribe, if necessary.

By the time the sky had lightened to a milky gray on my first morning in Si Saket, I was on a motorcycle taxi fleeing to the brightly lit hotel that I'd rejected the night before.

"Today where do you go?" the driver asked me.

"Khao Pra Viharn," I said. "Will you take me?"

"One hundred and twenty-five miles." His eyebrows shot up. "Take the bus."

"I hate buses. On motorcycles you can see everything. How much?"

And we agreed on a thousand baht.

Ponsak dropped me off at the Prom Phiman Hotel and returned at ten, looking dubious.

"Are you wearing those shoes?" he asked, eyes fixed on my high-heeled sandals. "Don't you have jeans?"

"I don't like them. It's okay. I can ride like this," and I tucked my skirt under my side-saddled legs, as I'd been taught in Bangkok.

He looked back, nodded, and we were on the highway.

The road took us through flat, open fields that were a waterless ocean under an unbroken sweep of sky. Grassland held haystacks that looked like giant wasp nests, small temples that were Grecianly chaste in their simplicity, and trees that were so picturesquely placed that it seemed as though they had been positioned by a landscape architect. Emerald green rice paddies were contained by borders as precise as picture frames, and a huge pond filled with lotus touched the horizon.

The road began to climb, winding up through outcroppings of rock and clumps of pine trees. Sunlight broke through the pewter clouds, and the sky brightened. We slowed down at the Thai checkpoint near the Thai/Khmer border, where a line of trucks waited for inspection. I clutched my bag that held my passport and money, ready to display both, but an impatient officer waved us through without hesitation.

"They don't think you're a tourist," Ponsak grinned as we sailed past what could have been a bureaucratic nightmare.

We reached a dusty parking lot at the end of the steep hill climb, and stood waiting for the vehicle that would carry me from the parking lot to the path that would bring me to the Cambodian border.

"Do you want to come?" I asked.

"No, I'll stay here and sleep. Are you afraid?"

"No, but I don't think I can go," I replied, worried that the border sentries would turn me back without an official receipt from the Thai checkpoint.

A quick ride ended at the edge of a forest, where a path through the trees warned that beyond the sanctioned route were landmines. A clearing and a stream marked the beginning of Cambodia, and smiling Khmer soldiers escorted me to a ticket seller.

Two hundred baht let me cross the border into a place that only a god could have imagined. Giant cobras flanked the entry, and slabs of quarried stone that were almost as long as my body cobbled the staircase that was carved into the cliff. Meadow grass, sprinkled with delicate, aspen-like trees, waved against signs cautioning that landmines were still a distinct possibility.

Five buildings broke the ascent at regular intervals, and entering their roofless walls gave the feeling that I was in the heart of a mountain. Their massive doorways were crowned with intricate, fading pictures carved into the rock. Halfway up, in the adjoining meadow, was a small recently constructed shelter with a smashed plane lying in pieces beside it. Beyond that reminder of modern death and war, the cliff and sky lured me away from the staircase. The rustling of leaves and grass was all that could be heard as I walked over earth that could harbor mines and felt nothing but benediction.

The final structure at the top of the stairs led to a temple, a tiny room that held a statue of the Buddha. Here a monk from Phnom Penh blessed visitors in Pali, while sprinkling them with water and striking their prostrate backs with three light blows from a little switch. Beside the temple, covered stone passageways led me down a geometrically straight hall to the edge of the world. Cambodia stretched below the cliff, brilliantly green, with Angkor Wat only another 60 miles in the distance. Surrounded by the windblown grass and the infinite stretch of sky, I shivered in the heat, knowing I was standing on sacred ground.

Hours later, back in my comfortable hotel room in Si Saket, I listened to a Wagnerian thunderstorm that Ponsak had outrun like a hell-spawned bat. As it crashed, I pictured lightning flashes on the walls of Khao Prah Viharn and knew that when I died, I wanted my ashes to become part of the wind that has blown against it for centuries.

19 ALL DRESSED UP WITH NO PLACE TO GO

It's dangerous, I soon discovered, for women to walk in Bangkok. A quick jaunt to pick up a newspaper began innocently enough and ended by coming home with a bunch of roses, two pairs of shoes, the perfect black skirt—and of course the newspaper. I never knew what I was going to find, since neighborhood vendors appeared and dissolved with no discernable pattern or schedule. The rule was if I saw it and it was right, grab it or forever mourn the loss. All was impermanence in the floating world of street shopping.

Shopping closely follows eating as Bangkok's favorite pastime, and it's a far less restrictive activity than in the States. Give Thai people an inch and they'll make a market, which is why walking down any street in this city is both fascinating and an obstacle course. Stalls on either side of a pedestrian thoroughfare, coupled with an ocean of pedestrians, give the Thainglish term *footpath* much more accuracy than "sidewalk."

It's possible to buy anything from food to auto parts on a Bangkok street. Shopping here is an act of serendipity, the art of finding something while looking for something else. It's true that it's easier, more direct, and more comfortable to go straight to a department store, but where's the fun in that? Shopping on the street took me back to a world of hunting and gathering. If I were meant to have it, I would find what I was looking for. If not, it would show up some other time in a spot where I least expected to find it.

As a short woman who suffered years of shopping indignities in the States, I found my revenge here. While my tall, long-legged friends searched and cursed and paid department store prices for the few items of clothing that would cover their height, I was deliriously grabbing skirts and slacks that didn't need to be taken up, and shoes that looked fabulous for five dollars a pair, and stockings that never bagged at the ankles.

The downside was finding something that didn't make me look like a walking shrine to Hello Kitty. The pure joy was that when I finally found something that wasn't pastel, or ruffled, or bowed, I knew it was going to fit.

So there I was, with half a dozen pairs of shoes that would make Manolo Blahnik sob with envy and a closet filled with clothes that I loved, and enough glittery, sparkly makeup to illuminate Las Vegas. Now what? Since Bangkok has deposed Manhattan as the city that never sleeps, I dressed up in my most satisfying outfit and I got into a taxi and I went out alone.

I was alone because I didn't want to go with a horde of other people and homestead a table in a club and drain a couple of bottles of whiskey while listening to pop music and classic disco hits. I'd learned that I had a choice between succumbing to the will of the majority or doing what I liked by myself. So, being an independent sort, I did precisely what I liked again and again and again until I was ready to sell my eyelashes for the company of just one person who liked to do what I did.

Overseas friends came and visited and went back home, leaving me with the uncomfortable knowledge that I liked what I did better when I did it with someone else who liked it too. But my straight male friends liked the girl-bars, and my gay male friends liked the boy-bars, and my female friends….

Since I'd rather have showered in boiling oil than go out with a group of other women, I had no idea what they liked to do, and I felt queasy at the thought of finding out. I had seen groups of expat females, traveling in whale pods, exuberant and jovial and having way, way too much fun, like overgrown children trick-or-treating in Disneyland. My Thai female friends, on the rare occasions that they ventured out after dark, sat in a cluster of isolated beauty, immobile and formal, like a reenactment of *Night of the Living Dead*. Both scenarios were the stuff, I told myself, that bad acid trips were made of.

As was the memorable night that I went with a large circle of Thai friends to the nightclub ghetto at Royal City Avenue, entered one of the neon caverns, and sat in a room so packed with stools and small, round, high tables that it was only possible to dance in our designated three inches of space. The ladies' room was crowded with extremely young girls who were vomiting into every available receptacle and later could be seen face down on wet and dirty tabletops. My white jacket never recovered from a fall onto the beer-soaked floor, solidifying my belief that black was better, and that going out alone meant the ability to leave before bad music did bad things to formerly good people. Stripped of that freedom, I stayed with my friends, flashing a rictus of counterfeit enjoyment and wondering if hell could possibly be any worse than this. We couldn't leave until a missing member of our party was found, enviably asleep in the peaceful darkness of the parking garage.

It was okay, though. I learned to be really good at entering a room by myself and listening to music that made me come alive and having a swell time, until the night that I got dressed up, and I looked in the mirror, and the woman who looked back at me refused to walk out the door.

I was middle-aged and I liked loud rock and roll and independent movies, and I believed that anyone who put soft drinks in their Scotch should be shot long before sunrise and I was female and I lived in Bangkok and I understood Eleanor Rigby far too well. I peered into my closet and I saw my empty suitcases and I knew there was a plane waiting for me with an offer that I was almost ready to accept, just as soon as I found the perfect traveling outfit that was waiting for me, out on the sidewalk, on the footpath, somewhere in this city.

20 DROWNING IN THE DEEP END

Living in Bangkok had become easy. At first I was wildly in love with the city, but that changed to a cozy marital relationship as I settled into a suburban neighborhood, with a comfortable apartment and a job that took up much of my time. I no longer wandered for hours, meandering through markets, or enjoying the contrast of real Louis Vuitton bags in a luxury mall with convincing replicas for sale inches away on the street, or watching temples blaze gold and scarlet against deep indigo twilight.

I spoke enough Thai to get around and to gain the injudicious praise of people who lie to be kind. I'd traveled successfully by myself, with my limited language skills and my hard-won knowledge of Thai behavior codes. I was, I felt, adequately assimilated and thoroughly at home in my chosen country.

As New Year's and its long holiday break approached, I didn't relish the thought of watching the year turn, alone, and when Ess, our friend, invited Rodney and me to go with him to his home in the country, I accepted gratefully.

Drawing up a small itinerary, I anticipated hiring a boat to Ayuttaya, looking for fabric in a nearby village market, and skydiving from a hot-air balloon at an accommodating army camp. As an independent traveler, I knew if my companions weren't enthusiastic about these plans, I could take a bus or a motorcycle taxi to go there by myself. In less active moments, I thought, I'd read or write in the restful quiet of rural Thailand.

Ess's house was deep in the country, and the drive took us away from the flat plains of central Thailand, high into the hills of Saraburi. It was nighttime, and the stars were huge and exhilarating. The darkness was alive with fires, burning away the stalks of last season's harvested crops. The road snaked farther and farther up, and away from any place I had ever been or seen. Sleepy and passive in the back seat, I stared into the smoke and starlight and marveled at the silence and isolation that we drove through.

I had become accustomed to the ugly noise and glare and unceasing motion of Bangkok. My apartment view looked over the expressway, where cars rushed by during every waking moment, including my insomniac hours. Bangkok's hyperactive roar and bustle had seemed to become part of my pulse, an unnoticed, essential fact of life.

The quiet flicker of light in the small towns punctuated the highway darkness that we were traveling through. The neon streets of the city seemed a lifetime behind us when we finally reached Ess's house, which was filled with sacks of dried corn and smelled like a hayloft, musty and sweet.

An impressive number of people, all related to Ess, came to help us open his house. Within a very short time, the corn sacks were moved to a corner of the main room, the floor was swept and mopped, and shutters were pushed outward to let in air that was clear, fresh, and almost cold.

In the group of relatives was a wiry lady who looked so elderly that I was sure she must be Ess's grandmother but who turned out to be his aunt. She had terrifying energy for her age, and I rushed to help her as she unearthed heavy stacks of sleeping pads and blankets and pillows. We talked briefly, and I almost understood her before everyone returned home, and we went to have dinner at a place where, once again, everybody was related to Ess.

This included a truly ancient woman who sat near us, chewed betel, expectorated blood-red spit, and was frankly skeptical when Ess assured her that I was a woman. My cropped hair and jeans were clearly male characteristics to her, no matter how much I smiled and fluttered my blue mascara-laden eyelashes in her direction.

Early the next day we were greeted by many of the people we had met the night before. They clustered and chattered and hovered until it became evident that the only personal relationship that we wanted in the morning was with many cups of strong coffee. They drifted away, and Ess got ready for work, helping his brother with an underground lottery business.

Fifty people scoured the area on motorcycles and bicycles, collecting three digit numbers and the money that was placed on these numbers. The numerical combinations and the names of those who had bet on them were transcribed on a list. When the official government lottery results were revealed, the list was checked to see if any of the three digit combinations corresponded with the final three digits of the winning numerals. If there was a match, money was paid out to the person who selected the lucky numbers. If not, Ess's brother kept the total take, paying the number collectors, the talliers, and the local police, since this was ostensibly illegal.

Rodney and I were torpid, only rousing from vacation mode to search for food, English language newspapers containing crossword puzzles, and shoes to replace my thin-strapped high heels, which had snapped from the shock of walking on unpaved ground. A small covered shelter down the road had fabulous noodles, as well as a collection of people who greeted us happily and knowledgeably, since they were all related to Ess. Hordes of muscular chickens milled around the table, watching us eat one of their tribe, and a woman who had smiled at us carried a rather nasty-looking scythe away with her when she finished her lunch. "Thank God she liked us," Rod observed as she walked past.

The newsstands that are everywhere in Bangkok were invisible here.

We stopped and consulted with Ess who looked doubtful but suggested a neighboring town. Driving through fields of small and vibrant sunflowers, we reached a sizable outpost whose sidewalks and small buildings attested to the success of the local cement industry. The shops were overflowing with New Year's presents, many already wrapped and labeled with a price, but bearing no clue as to the contents. Feeling I needed a more personal retail experience, I bought a clock for Ess, which was embellished with a figure of a man whose arm twitched spasmodically as he tried to launch a bowling ball into what looked very much like a toilet. This was the high point of our shopping excursion, since not only were there no newspapers that we could read, there were also no shoes that didn't resemble rubber shower slippers. Gloomily and companionably sharing a large bottle of beer, we drove back to our books and inertia. Ess soon joined us with a bad case of writer's cramp from a day of writing down numbers, and the news that it had been a bad day for his brother. There had been a winner who walked away with 200,000 baht, or about $4,650. In spite of the loss, his brother was going to buy us dinner, which he would deliver soon.

Rod and I were deep in the agonies of an unsolvable crossword puzzle from an *International Herald Tribune* that I'd fortunately brought with me, but we stopped cursing long enough to shower for our impending guest. This involved repeated sluicing from large jars of amazingly cold water, while standing on planks outdoors, contemplating a field of dried cornstalks and the dramatically rocky hills on the horizon. Getting clean while clad modestly in a sundress was a challenge but less of one than if I had been showering while struggling to remain covered with a sarong. Women in the country do this without a qualm, but it is not a skill that is fostered by living in a Bangkok apartment.

Ess's brother brought enough food for a regiment, which arrived soon after he did. The decrepit aunt from the night before was prominent among the cluster of family who joined us, and she was definitely a woman who could keep a conversation going. Her English skills consisted of an abrupt and peremptory "You!" that she used to preface long, rapid, and frequently intimate questions in Thai. As the brother alternately wished us Happy New Year and told us exactly how much dinner had cost, the aunt interrogated us Americans about our homes in the States and stateside employment opportunities for the able-bodied males of her family. The juxtaposition of subjects proved unnerving over the long haul. Rodney developed a deep interest in the fire that Ess had built by igniting dried corncobs and retreated to study the flames. I took solace in flirting with a little girl who was one of Ess's cousins, winning smiles from her while constructing moronic pleasantries in very bad Thai, struggling to understand the convoluted sentences that were fired at me by a long succession of family members, and feeling very much out of my depth.

We foreigners avoided an early morning wedding ceremony that was scheduled on the following day and relapsed into taciturnity and huge quantities of caffeine. I tried to walk closer to the surrounding hills, crunching through corn stalks and delicate empty husks, wondering if the hard kernels under my feet would pop as the morning sun grew hotter. Barbed wire fences turned me back to the road, which led to a lovely little lake with a thick border of nettles. I was nursing my stings and watching the sun glitter on the water when Ess drove up. Marveling at the length of my quarter-mile trek, he whisked me into the car to get his grandmother and go to an aunt's house for a New Year's celebration.

His grandmother was gracious, lovely, tiny, and heavily addicted to chewing betel. "She always has it in her mouth. If she forgets to bring it with her, we have to go back and get her basket," Ess told me. My heart sank. I'd had incomprehensible chats before with women whose mouths were filled with a few teeth and a lot of betel. These encounters were most charitably described as difficult. They usually ended with the old woman, thoroughly bored with my nods and smiles and unintelligible responses, stumping away with the knowledge that I was a blithering half-wit. And sure enough, Ess's grandmother and I soon agreed to a silent amicability, since neither of us had a clue as to what the other was saying.

Ess's aunt's house lay far beyond the lake and closer to the hills that were apparently cordoned off with barbed wire. Tables were filled with food and beer and many, many relatives. The garrulous, inquisitive aunt arrived and, learning that she was seven years my junior, alternated between bellows of "You!" and "*Pi*" (older sister) to continue our fascinating dialogue. More family drove in from Bangkok with bottles of Chivas Regal, and everybody settled in for a long day of eating, drinking, and chatting.

Ess and Rod became embroiled in a vicious game of poker, and I joined a boy who was watching Thai boxing on TV. This action was highly amusing to all, and a few voices merrily speculated that I was a tomboy, which is Thainglish for *lesbian*. The boy who had been sitting nearby faded away, and I sat alone, watching two men kick the shit out of each other, feeling like a leper of questionable gender.

I wandered outside, where the conversation was faster than I could fathom and the wind was blowing hard enough to whisk the tops off the ice buckets. Deciding I'd look for a break in the barbed-wire barrier and an access route to the hills, I began to search for the rubber shower slippers that Ess had presented to me the day before. Spread outside the house were at least a dozen pairs of slippers that were identical to mine, and as I slipped some on, many people were ready with assurances that they didn't belong to me.

Barefoot, I walked to the corner of the house and squatted in the sun. Surrounded by words that I was tired of struggling to understand and by people who were related to everyone but two people in the immediate vicinity, I felt more alone than I ever had in any of my solitary travels. I didn't know which province I was in; I didn't know where the nearest bus or train station was; I didn't know where the nearest motorcycle taxi stand was. Hell, I didn't even know where my shower slippers were. To my horror, tears began to roll below the protective barrier of my sunglasses and my only wish was to go back to my cozy Bangkok apartment.

Slowly I got myself under control, and slowly I found my purse and a pair of slippers I was almost sure were mine. And very slowly I sauntered off to the road and began to walk away.

"I want to go home," I told Rodney when he found me sitting outside Ess's locked house. There was no public transportation in that corner of the world, but some of the guests were going back to the closest large town and took me with them. As I boarded the bus that would return me to Bangkok, I knew that it was my first step on a much longer journey that would return me to a small place in the world where everybody was related to me.

21 SKYTRAIN TOURISTS

Bangkok during the last half of the 1990s was a gigantic construction zone, a crazy salad of heavy equipment, excavation, concrete girders, and laborers who appeared to be at work twenty-four hours a day. Traffic continued to inch past on each side of the project, which provided a welcome note of interest for those who found themselves stuck in an unmoving mass of vehicles for a couple of hours.

The cranes and bulldozers were often painted in a lovely shade of turquoise, and the workers seemed to be having a good time. It was always fun to watch them taking a lunch break, as they sprawled among massive chunks of concrete and mountains of excavated clay, eating and laughing and drinking beer. It was one of the happiest and lengthiest building projects that I, the daughter of an Alaskan construction worker, had ever seen, and although it was reputed that someday all of this jolly chaos would result in a citywide monorail, to a casual onlooker that seemed dubious.

Eventually the girders were in place like gigantic dead trees, casting deep shadows on the streets below, and in some amazing way were connected by miles of tracks that seemed to float above the city. On the King's birthday, the inaugural train took potentates and dignitaries on a whirlwind trip through Bangkok, and we peasants gaped at the idea of traveling from one side of our traffic-clogged city to the other in a matter of minutes.

Bangkok is a city that may not have invented the traffic jam, but it certainly has perfected it into an art form. Early in my teaching career,

I took my first truly death-defying motorcycle taxi ride when Rod's car had been stationary for half an hour and there was a class expecting us in fifteen minutes. "Take a motorcycle, start the class, and I'll join you when this lets up," he promised. He never showed up, and I got home three hours later to find that he'd preceded my arrival to our neighborhood by ten minutes.

That was how I learned that owning a car in Bangkok meant that, like a captain of a sinking ship, you had to stay with it no matter what, that to be on time for an appointment meant leaving two hours in advance, and that, when you were on a traffic-jammed bus, it was wise to start looking for the closest motorcycle taxi stand. These were truths as inexorable as the law of gravity until the Skytrain began to run, changing how people went and, as it turned out, where.

I had loved exploring Bangkok, taking buses to far-flung neighborhoods both for work and for pleasure, but a typical Thai workweek consists of six days. With a whole twenty-four hours to squander on errands and recreation, a four-hour roundtrip bus ride ate up a substantial portion of a weekend. The Skytrain took a fraction of that time, and it was spotlessly clean and cold enough to chill beer.

It followed a shopper's route, linking every upscale boutique mall in the city, on all of the major commercial thoroughfares. It so completely divorced its passengers from the life of the street, which is the true heart of Bangkok, that I once spent an entire gloomy, soggy Songkran weekend high and dry on the Skytrain to avoid the exuberant citywide water fight that characterizes Thai New Year in April.

I loved the efficiency of the Skytrain and was seduced by its speed, even though I found the uniformity of its journeys mind-deadeningly dull. It whisked me high above streets that had enchanted me with unexpected visual treasures: a market stall that sold whole pig's heads, a pen of goats tucked away near the city's luxurious riverside hotels, an orchid seller providing a wild splash of color in the middle of a concrete monotone of gray, a beauty shop with the charmingly unenticing English name of Hairface.

Later, when I no longer lived in Bangkok and returned as a yearly visitor, I saw more of my fellow-foreigners on one Skytrain ride than I had in the city during all of my years as a resident, and with good reason. When I was learning my way around that demented city, I would have loved the Skytrain. That I would never have learned what I knew about Bangkok, to a traveler would seem decidedly beside the point; the important thing was it made Bangkok user-friendly to people who had no intention of staying beyond a week or two.

On the Skytrain it is possible to explore the city without getting lost, and although I stoutly maintain that getting lost is the best form of exploration, few map-carrying, schedule-bound travelers would agree with me. From the most luxurious hotels; to the fabulous Weekend Market with its merchandise from every corner of the Kingdom and beyond; to the affluent shopping centers at Siam Square where Ferrari and Versace and Cartier wait in palatial surroundings for those who can afford them and for those who like to dream; to the Chao Phraya riverboats that go to the Grand Palace and Wat Arun—places that all were accessible by expensive and traffic-crippled taxis a few years ago are now reached rapidly, comfortably, and with very little confusion in this air-conditioned, bilingual conveyance. Shops near the ticket booths at the entrance sell drinks and snacks in hygienic and comprehensible surroundings and nobody addresses foreigners as "You!" or "Madame" as they rush by to catch the train. The stops are announced both in English and in Thai, and far enough in advance that maps can be consulted and members of groups can be assembled for disembarkation. It's convenient, it's clean, it's scam-free, and it keeps culture shock at bay. It takes travelers in a hermetically sealed environment to scenes from the city's most popular postcards. It may be, although I devoutly hope it's not, the harbinger of Bangkok's future—safe, sterile, and regulated.

Perhaps the best thing about the Skytrain is that its territory is limited. It's a wonderful way to take care of all the niggling errands that intrude upon a vacation: going to a currency-exchange, buying presents for the folks back home, getting aspirin and shampoo and English language books and magazines. Best of all, it leads to Victory Monument, the dizzying traffic circle that is the rallying point for almost every bus in the city. There it's possible to puzzle out which bus will take you to Ramkhamhaeng, the university neighborhood with miles of trendy clothing stalls and great cheap food, or Pattanakan Road with its wonderful Northeastern Thai papaya salad and grilled chicken places, or the Huay Kwang market, with its fresh food and cheap clothes and bright plastic housewares, which is one of my favorite places in the city. Or sometimes it's fun just to jump on a bus at random and take it to unknown territory, to the edge of the world, where there be dragons and adventures and Thailand truly begins.

22 GOING HOME AGAIN

I should have remembered Thomas Wolfe when I was planning my visit to Bangkok. "You'd be bored stiff," I explained to friends who claimed to wish they were going with me, "I'm going to my other home for two weeks; it won't be exciting. I'm going to stay in the apartment building that I used to live in; I'm going to eat in my old neighborhood; I'm going to see friends. I'm just going to do what I did when I lived there."

I didn't pack for this trip by trying to stuff my life into two suitcases, the way I always used to do when returning to Thailand to live and work after time spent in the States. I had never gone back with a shopping list before, and I went to the airport with a weird little cluster of tension in my neck rather than with my customary wild jubilation over leaving the old country for the home I had chosen. I'd been gone for a record absence of four years, and I was only going to be in Bangkok for a little while.

I got on the plane feeling as though a meeting with an old boyfriend were looming in my future, with that strange mixture of anticipation and dread. Somewhere in the back of my mind was the fear that once I got to Thailand, I might abandon the life that I had so carefully reconstructed in the States.

What I didn't expect was that during my four years in the USA I had turned back into an American.

I had worked so hard to become a resident of Thailand, the kind of foreigner who learned to accept, if not love, every aspect of my new surroundings, and who blended in as well as my oversized nose would allow. I'd learned to walk at a snail's pace, to use toothpicks behind a shielding hand after every meal, to look at diseased dogs without visible disgust, and to do my damndest to behave like a well-mannered, reserved lady when in public. Most important of all, I had a slot in my neighborhood. I was a teacher and a person who worked the same demanding, ridiculous schedule that almost every Thai person does, from the crack of dawn until late at night, six days a week.

Everything that I did and saw was filtered through that schedule. On my way to work perched on the back of a motorcycle in the early morning, I watched—immaculate, starched-and-ironed, navy blue and white uniforms on the bodies of children who were packed into the backs of pickup trucks to go to school; barefoot monks receiving food from a long line of women who spooned out meals from the large baskets that they carried; a placid parade of big white oxen lumbering down the side of a road to reach the bordering field—and was always delighted by what I saw, even after I'd stopped being surprised. Walking to a class in a Muslim neighborhood, I'd stop dead in my tracks to listen to the call to prayer from a mosque that was silhouetted against a darkening violet sky. I loved the hiss and sizzle of the pink and blue and green lightsaber neon tubes that switched on at sunset to illuminate carts of noodles or soup or rice or squid or roses.

I learned to enjoy things that came inadvertently and to savor them quickly while on my way to where I needed to be. Small kindnesses lit up my world, and a conversation in English was so infrequent that it would sustain me for a week. "What a boring life you have," an expat acquaintance once told me, but my existence was illuminated by incidental pleasures.

This was what I thought I would return to on my two-week visit, but my vacationer's schedule proved to be an obstacle to my goal of resuming the life that I had missed during my US exile. In all the years I'd lived in

Bangkok, I'd never been there with the leisure and the disposable cash that I brought with me on this two-week vacation. Usa was horrified at the number of taxis that I took when we were together, and steered me toward the slow and crowded buses whenever she could. "I'm afraid you're spending too much money," she said repeatedly, and part of me stood back and remembered how I took pride in forgoing taxis for buses, but the truth was I didn't have the patience for them any more. That was a sad fact of life because the buses were where I learned much of what I knew about Thailand.

It was on the buses that I learned to surrender my bags and bundles while standing next to seated people who smiled and beckoned for me to place my burden on their laps, and where I learned to offer the same courtesy when I was the one who was sitting. I saw and imitated people who stood to give their seats to schoolchildren and to the elderly and to mothers with children. I began to move back as far as I could on a crowded bus and made my body as small as possible while putting my huge book bag between my feet as I stood, often for hours, packed among bodies that always smelled clean.

The buses were so slow that I could window shop when I was on them, studying the Walt Disney Cinderella wedding gowns in the shops on Paholyothin Road, choosing a couch from the furniture shops on the grimy sidewalks of Lat Phrao, deciding which stall had the freshest roses near Saphan Kwai. I saw things I wasn't meant to see, like the murky interiors of the blowjob bars on Suttisan Road, in the daytime when they were clearing out the smell of stale beer and dead cigarettes for the next round of customers. I discovered that the exteriors of "coffee shops" were festooned with pictures of pretty young women, not of cappuccinos and caffe lattes. I never saw children crying.

I listened to conversations shamelessly on buses, trying to understand words or to hear the tones that I never failed to mispronounce. I mapped the city from bus windows, finding new areas to walk through when I had the time. I had hated the buses and I had loved them and I had spent two-thirds of my Thai life riding them. Now, as an American visitor, I took taxis and the Skytrain and the subway. I took the time to ride the bus twice and each time I felt very out of place.

I was out of place in my old neighborhood also, although people were too polite to make me feel that way. Instead they asked me where my family was, why my sons weren't traveling with me, and why didn't I come with friends. Old ladies lavished me with kindly attention that made me twitch, assuring me every day that my clothes were beautiful and asking me where I was going and what I would do when there. Vacationers don't usually come to that part of Bangkok, and the strain of having one in their midst was a huge responsibility, even when it was a vacationer with a familiar face. After the day that one of the friendly noodle-stall owners tried to set me up with a teaching job, I began to leave quite early in the morning and to return after dark to avoid running the gauntlet of concerned curiosity.

There are so many things I miss about Bangkok, and I've been planning my next trip ever since I got back to the States after this last visit. Next time I'll know enough to know that I'm traveling, not stepping back into an old life. I'll stay in a hotel; I'll travel outside of the city; I'll have an itinerary that I just might stick to. But still, I'll do all of that with the knowledge of how it felt, a few years ago, to ride behind a motorcycle driver, watching the late afternoon sun sparkle on the lake at Beung Khum where men sit beneath the trees, smoking and fishing for their suppers

ADVENTURE

23 A FEW OF MY FAVORITE THINGS

Visiting Bangkok is a strange experience for me, a tangled time that's filled with a mingling of the self-indulgence of a vacationer and the yearning for the life I had when I made my home there. I eat and shop and spend time with friends, while looking back on days when I had no time or money for those pleasures, but was nourished by the deep joy of always learning something new. During my vacation, I try to spend my visits in areas that are frequented by residents of the city, not by travelers, which helps me to avoid the touts, the miles of mass-produced kitsch, and the over-exposed attractions that make many foreign guests flee the city as rapidly as possible.

Thonburi is the Brooklyn of Bangkok, over a bridge and well away from the glitz, and for that reason I like it. The Grand Tower Inn is my hotel, a stone's throw from the river and the Pepsi Pier, where commuter boats whisk me across the Chao Phraya and to the Skytrain in minutes. It's not a glamorous place by any means, but the rooms are comfortable and clean, the dining room is a good place to wake up over a pot of instant coffee that is elegantly served, and the staff members are friendly, helpful, and speak better English than I do Thai.

Thonburi is full of stunning temples that are much less crowded than their Bangkok counterparts, canals that are still navigable and well-used, and little markets with fresh fruit and flowers and food and shoes and handbags that are dirt-cheap and fabulous. It is a place that looks far less interesting than it actually is, and, although it boasts more than a few McDonald's, there's not yet a Starbucks in sight.

I love to shop but I'm not a bargainer; the result always seems worth much less than the amount of time it takes to achieve it. I go to neighborhoods where the price will be low, and then I pay it. Sometimes I get a sympathy discount from the vendor, on the grounds that since I was too stupid to ask for one, I definitely need some sort of help, but that's generosity they have given, not a favor that I ask for. I go to the shopping extravaganzas of Silom, Sukhimvit, and Siam Square because that's where the bookstores are, but other than buying vast amounts of reading material that I can only find in Bangkok at Bookazine, Asia Books, Kinokuniya, and Dasa Books, I rarely spend much time there.

On the Skytrain route, Victory Monument is only minutes away from any of the tourist streets, and it's a mecca for those who love good food. It's also a shopping area for girls, so everything is made in miniscule sizes. My only successful purchases there are shoes and handbags, and sometimes there's something pretty to wear in one of the few old ladies' clothing stalls, which are the only places where I can find clothes that will fit me.

The best places to eat, in my prejudiced opinion, are near the fresh markets, because people who sell the ingredients are the ones who are going to eat there. Seafood at night on Yaowarat Road is pure heaven—every mouthful is delicious and sitting outside in that blaze of neon and traffic is like having dinner on the set for *Blade Runner*.

The Sikh neighborhood on Chakraphet Road has great Indian food and the cheapest underwear in the world. I stock up for a year for twenty-five dollars and have lunch afterwards at Royal India—their garlic *naan* is what I'll eat every day after I die, if I'm good in this life. It's also where my best Thai female friend buys fabric to take to her seamstress, but that's not for amateur shoppers like me, unless I go with Usa. The sari shops are tempting, and I know I'll succumb and buy one someday, but only when I'm ancient enough to have the presence to carry it off.

I never know where cute shoes are going to show up, but when they do, if they're in my size, I grab them. Favorite spots are in the University district of Ramkhamhang Road, on the fringes of Victory Monument, and at the insanity of small shops on the ground floor of Mahboonkrong Shopping Center near Siam Square.

The riverboat trip to Nonthaburi is one of my best-loved activities, and the market there has lovely wooden spoons of all sizes and salad servers and bowls, all beautifully shaped and burnished to a gleaming finish, which are fun to take home as presents for friends. Lunch by the river is something I always have time for; the setting is so spectacular that I eat whatever I order without any kind of inward criticism. Besides, there's usually a small resident cat to help me dispose of whatever I want to give.

Chatuchak Market is the best place to find clothes that will fit farang-sized bodies—I've found real treasures in the stalls that sell second-hand clothing from other countries and the T-shirt stalls are always good for a few laughs. A T-shirt of Che Guevara that was emblazoned "Charlie" has proved to be unforgettable. "Go early, go often" is my motto for visiting Chatuchak—it's worth heading out there early to avoid the heat and the crowds, and it's so huge and labyrinthine that more than one trip is essential. If something looks good, stop and check it out, because you'll never find it again, even with a compass, a map, and GPS equipment. I don't like to eat at Chatuchak though—it's too crowded and busy for me to be able to enjoy the food there.

In the old part of the city, I love to visit the lovely little bronze horses at Wat Suthat near the Giant Swing; neighboring Wat Rajabhopit, with its dazzling exterior of tiles that look like kaleidoscope patterns of Persian splendor; and Suksit Siam, the bookshop founded by the activist firebrand Sulak Sivalak, which has a generous helping of life-changing books in English, and which to me is Bangkok's true Democracy Monument.

I love it when I approach Chinatown because that's where I invariably become wildly disoriented. There's always someone who can help me get my bearings again, but I'm never in a rush to lose the dizzy feeling of unknowing that comes with aimless roaming. I come away with questions about what I've seen ("What ailment is cured by those dried seahorses in the pharmacies?") and the deep happiness that comes from a small adventure.

Bangkok is a city that bulges with small adventures and large kindnesses, which can be found in a heartbeat if you leave your guidebook in your hotel room and avoid the spots where entrepreneurial souls address you in English. Come with me, we'll have a wonderful time.

"CATCH FIRE; KINDLE

24 FIREWEED AND JASMINE

My father ran through darkness toward a house that was filled with fire. My mother, standing on a snow-covered Alaskan hill, held her children in her burned arms and shrieked his name.

My parents lost everything they owned that night, in a scene that was vividly impressed on my four-year-old memory. As I grew older, my initial lesson of fear was replaced by the deeper one of impermanence. I learned that possessions could be lost and lives altered in a flicker of time, and that a house is as secure as a soap bubble.

Our fire took us away from the tree-ringed lake that we'd lived beside and loved. My father and I would return occasionally to gather water lilies for my mother, armloads of strange, waxy flowers that smelled fresh, not sweet. We'd walk through the dense, green darkness of a spruce forest, which opened to a clear hill with a view of sun-sparkled water. Knowing that this hill was the one where my mother had stood with us and screamed only made me feel that it belonged to my family. I would send my small voice over the lake to greet the other voice that lived on the opposite side, another little girl whose strange and lovely name came back to me as I called, "Echo."

This was our place, I knew. I'd absorbed it through the soles of my bare feet. It was years before I understood that we'd never live there again. Long after I knew that my parents had given up the trees, the lake, and

the water lilies, I still thought of them as ours, and learned that owner-
ship was both intrinsic and impermanent.

It was an animist world that I chose to live in. I distrusted houses; in my
dreams they broke to pieces or sheltered skeletons who had taken the
place of my parents and sisters. At night I lay awake, protecting my family, listening for the sound of flames. I felt safest when I was outdoors,
and that's where I spent most of my time.

I studied the shadow and motion and the gold-green shimmer of spruce
boughs while lying on a hill of moss, staring through the tree branches
at the sky and longing to taste the clouds. There was a peace that came
from doing this, a contented quiet that I remembered immediately
when I later read, "Be still and know that I am God."

The same feeling came when I sat alone and watched the passage of
the river, or walked through grass as tall as I was, unbroken by trails or
houses, or came upon strange clearings surrounded by groves of trees,
with light slanting through thick branches in shafts that looked solid but
eluded touch. Other spots were dreadful for no reason; I'd leave them
quickly and then avoid them.

I was forbidden to cross the river alone, and I did, every chance I got.
There the meadows were large and welcoming, with small belts of trees
that were stunted and dark and felt threatening when I walked past
them. When I was an adolescent and thought briefly about suicide,
those trees were, I decided, where I would choose to die.

Taught to believe in souls, I attributed the different atmospheres of these
places to the souls of trees, grass, and the river. Living far from church-
es, I found them in the world that I walked through, and I learned to
take my sadness and my fears to private, natural sanctuaries. My prayers
were silent ones, and my god wasn't found in Baby Jesus's crèche, or
bleeding on a cross. It was nonspecific, and it was in everything I saw,
when I walked away from our house.

That was a turbulent place that belonged to my parents, with treacherous terrain. I yearned to leave it, but discovered when I did, that for me no house would ever seem secure or permanent.

It was strange for me to come to Bangkok, a city where nature has been smothered by cement, and find it was a place where multitudes of shrines pay homage to the souls of natural things. Bright scarves are wrapped around trees as offerings; moving water is honored with tiny boats laden with gifts of flowers, candles, and incense; little houses shelter the spirits that have been dispossessed by buildings; and everything material is recognized as being transitory.

"We only rent them," a friend explained about the Buddha images that Thai people wear on chains or cords around their necks, "We can not own them." Somewhere within me, a four-year-old girl listened, nodded in agreement, and felt at home.

JANET BROWN

Janet Brown has always lived on the Pacific Rim: in Alaska, Seattle, and Thailand. A bookseller for twenty years, she was until recently travel buyer at the Elliott Bay Book Company, that literary oasis that makes Seattle livable.

Janet took an extended cigarette break between 1995 and 2001 to teach English in Bangkok. She is now back in Seattle, reinventing her life and planning a permanent return to that city that she loves best in the world, despite her continuing battle with the Thai language (which up to this point is the clear-cut winner).

NANA CHEN

Nana Chen is an internationally published freelance photographer and writer whose work has appeared in Adbusters, South China Morning Post, Real Travel UK, and the in-flight magazines of Thai Airways, Scandinavian Airlines, China Airlines and other major airlines. She has made several guest appearances on the Travel Channel's Bizarre Foods with Andrew Zimmern and contributed to art columns for the Council for Cultural Affairs Taiwan and South China Morning Post's "World-Beat." Nana is currently based in Bangkok and continues to travel wherever work takes her.

www.NanaChen.com

To Vietnam With Love
A Travel Guide for the Connoisseur
Edited & with contributions by Kim Fay
Photographs by Julie Fay Ashborn

To North India With Love
A Travel Guide for the Connoisseur
Edited & with contributions by Nabanita Dutt
Photographs by Nana Chen

To Japan With Love
A Travel Guide for the Connoisseur
Edited & with contributions by Celeste Heiter
Photographs by Robert George

To Myanmar With Love
A Travel Guide for the Connoisseur
Edited & with contributions by Morgan Edwardson
Photographs by Steve Goodman

To Asia With Love
*A Connoisseur's Guide to Cambodia, Laos,
Thailand, & Vietnam*
Edited & with contributions by Kim Fay
Photography by Julie Fay

Vignettes of Japan
Fifty vignettes of an American's life in Japan
By Celeste Heiter
Photography by Robert George

Vignettes of Taiwan
*Short Stories, Essays & Random
Meditations About Taiwan*
By Joshua Samuel Brown

Strolling in Macau
A Visitor's Guide to Macau, Taipa, & Coloane
By Steven K. Bailey
Photography by Jill C. Witt